THE GRATITUDE ATTITUDE
- Life Lessons from the Field -

THE GRATITUDE ATTITUDE
- Life Lessons from the Field -

Written by
Sheila Trask

DEDICATION

This is a special dedication to **Dr. Wayne Dyer**, who passed during the writing of this book.

I am truly grateful for the wisdom, knowledge, and love that you have shared through your brilliant books and presentations. Since I first discovered your work there have been many nights that I listened to your voice as I drifted off to sleep. You helped me deal with pain and grief, and helped me find answers within for the many questions I had about life. You were truly a gift to this world. The most important thing you taught me was to believe in myself, so that my soul and not my earthly self would dictate what I would do with my time here on earth. I owe my transformation to you.

I AM… eternally grateful.
Sheila

FOREWORD

I am so grateful for the opportunity to share my thoughts about gratitude. I see adopting an attitude of gratitude as similar to experiencing a paradigm shift: things suddenly start looking and feeling different. This awakening opens up your life, letting you perceive opportunities you might not have noticed before.

In writing this book, Sheila Trask has given you a great gift: a way to develop a new, more joyful way of living in the world. The Gratitude Attitude will not only change the way you see things, it will change the way you get out of bed and start your day. If you're practicing an attitude of gratitude, you'll find that your back pack of life will get lighter with each passing day. It all begins with gratitude. The way you look at yourself and the world around you will change as you do. Your heart will grow lighter as you begin to see yourself and others in a more enlightened way.

Life is not about being free of pain or sorrow or other things that trouble us. But instead of dwelling on our troubles, we can learn to look for the positive in our lives. This book holds the key. A shift in your thinking, a shift in your attitude, will help you be grateful for who you are and for the people around you. As you read this book, page after page you will begin to see the signs of change in your life. People ask me how I find the courage to climb mountains. I tell them I like to live my life to the fullest. I am grateful for each and every day. I practice living in the present. I believe that by living in the now, I am open to being grateful for everything around me, even the smallest of things. I wake up every morning to another chance to live life, to experience my place in it, and all that goes on around me. I look forward to a chance to make a difference. That is what gives me courage.

There is a strong link between what I do on the mountains and the challenges that many young people face today. Life is a series of ups and downs, good days and bad days. It's a balance of knowing when to hold on and when to let go. Everything we experience is based on the choices we make. We need to make smart choices, trust ourselves, face our fears, take chances, and not be afraid to fail. We need to have the courage to fall down and the strength to get back up again. I see every day as a new opportunity, a new possibility. When we shift our way of thinking, we become grateful. When we feel gratitude, we begin to feel more positive and energetic, and our self-esteem grows. We feel fearless, like something inside of us has changed, and it grows as if the light within has been ignited by fuel. Everything around us becomes more positive; with a gratitude attitude, we attract positive people. Our lives can be changed forever, if we believe. It's important to believe in yourself. It's important to believe in your dreams.

With gratitude,
Al Hancock

Al Hancock

Al made Canadian history by ascending the peak of Mount Makalu in the spring of 2014. He followed that up in June with a successful climb of the extremely challenging K2, the world's second highest peak. On both occasions he served as Expedition Leader. To date, he's successfully scaled six of the world's 14 tallest mountains, all of them over 8,000 metres, including Everest twice. His plan, over the next three years, is to become the first Newfoundlander, the first Canadian, and the second North American, to summit all fourteen 8,000-metre peaks. Go to **www.alhancock.com** to learn more about Al's journey.

Over the past decade, Al Hancock has been quietly making Canadian history; now he wants to take his journey to a new level, backed by sponsors who are aligned with his values of adventure, exploration, passion, commitment, respect, and safety. If you would like to be one of those sponsors, please contact **al@alhancock.com.**

AL Hancock

- 1st Newfoundlander to summit Mt. Everest
- 1st Newfoundlander to complete the Seven Summits
- 13th Canadian to complete the Seven Summits (202nd worldwide)

SPECIAL THANKS

I would like to thank my childhood friend *Al Hancock* for writing the Foreword for this book. I am so proud of his accomplishments and so grateful that we've reconnected, after almost 40 years, to help each other follow our dreams. This universe never ceases to amaze me. I know Al will fulfill his dream to complete all 14 summits. He is truly an inspiration for everyone who believes in the power of dreams.

Thanks to my parents who are in the spirit world *(Effie and Gerard White)* for being my parents and always believing in me. I can still hear my mom saying, *"You can do anything you put your mind to."*
I would like to acknowledge the people who have helped me get this book off the ground. Thanks to *Amy Callahan* for assisting me by typing my handwritten notes. Thanks to *Lindsay Delaney* of **City Light Images** for my photo. You are a source of inspiration. My amazing friend and editor, *Gail Collins*, when our universes collide, watch out. I am truly grateful for you and your intent to make this book the best it can be. I would also like to thank my sister *Isabel* and her son *Craig* for being brave and taking the final look. And for the beautiful gratitude meditation, I thank *Judith Royle*. I am always grateful for you.

I would be negligent not to mention *Bob Proctor* and *Sandy Gallagher,* as it was through the **Matrixx** I attended in August 2015, that I found the courage to take this book off the shelf and complete it. The **Matrixx** allowed me to open up my creative portal, believe in myself, and bulldoze through to capture my goal. The encouragement and support I received from them, their staff, and the other participants is priceless. It was through the **Matrixx** that I met the amazing people that helped me get this book together. The incredible designer *Patty Knowles* had this great ability to share my vision, and she has captured it in the cover. I also met *Peggy McColl*, who through her **Millionaire Author Intensive Program** coached me through the book by providing me with the information I needed to complete and market it. She is amazing and supportive, a wealth of information. I am also grateful for the beautiful couple I met at the Matrixx, *Alejandro Torres Dumani* and *Kasia Dziurda*. I reached out to them and they were so forthcoming in their advice about marketing and layout. Their **Kindle Wealth Factory** is helping many people share their work with the world. I highly recommend all of these people. Lastly, to my Mastermind group leader *Ed Wheeler,* and my fellow **"Thinking Into Results"** consultants, I am so fortunate to have you in my life, even if most of the time it is virtual. You encourage me, drive me, challenge me, and, most importantly, you help me constantly move forward in the direction of my life's purpose. I am grateful.

To learn more about Judith Royle, her amazing meditations, and her trainings, please go to (www.royletreatmentwellness.com) and/or (www.soulgenesis.com).

The **Matrixx** is a 6-day live event with **Bob Proctor** of the **Proctor Gallagher Institute**. It is designed to allow a limited number of people to work directly on their goals, business-building objectives, challenges, and breakthroughs for more effective wealth creation and accumulation. The event only takes place in Toronto, Canada.

This book is for the greatest gift that God has given me:

My son,

Jacob Vaughn Trask

There is but one lesson that you must live by...

Always be Grateful

Mom

CONTENTS

PART I
- FINDING GRATITUDE -

"Gratitude makes sense of our past, brings peace for today, and creates a vision for tomorrow."

~ Melody Beattie

THE EVOLUTION OF LIFE LESSONS FROM THE FIELD

"I am grateful for the idea that has used me."

~ Alfred Adler

Life Lessons from the Field is a new series in which **The Gratitude Attitude** is the premier edition. It first began as an assignment for my leadership class in the winter of 2013. I decided to try a new approach that would teach students to think critically and allow them to practise their leadership skills. I asked the students to select a quote that spoke to them; write about it, relate it to their lives; present their thoughts to the class; and then engage the class in discussion. I gave each student a copy of the presentation and asked them to use a journal to record their thoughts about the quote, the presenter's interpretation, and the class discussion. I also asked each student to record five things they were grateful for. I wondered which quotes the students would choose, how they would interpret them, and if they would become more positive as a result of the assignment. I never imagined that the gratitude part of the assignment would take over. The simple act of recording the things they were grateful for began to change their attitudes and the dynamics in the classroom.

SHEILA TRASK

(You can find the original assignment at the end of this section.)

I presented a quote the first week, followed by a different student each week. Over the course of the semester, I watched the students change. They became more aware of how precious their time was in school. They started appreciating each other and their families and started complaining less throughout the day. I also noted that they became more tolerant of each other, more confident, and more self-aware. Most students started to get better grades and submit their work on time. They became happier, more contented students. I was really pleased to see how the students looked forward to each presentation. It turned out to be their favorite assignment. They enjoyed anticipating what the others would present and how they would apply the quote to their lives.

At the end of the semester they submitted their journals for grading. Reading the journals, I was amazed by what the students had written. I realized we needed to share this with the world. I asked the class if I could use their work to write a book that might help others by sharing what we had created.

As they say, "When the student is ready, the teacher will appear." And here I am throughout this book giving words of wisdom to my students. One of my international students always called me "Teacher" so I have adopted that persona for this book; it always made me smile and feel like I was a Zen master or a spiritual advisor of some sort.

It is our hope that others may take comfort from the wisdom in this book, that it may give them inspiration to view their lives in a more positive way, and help them find gratitude for everything—big and small—in their lives. You see, "Life is how you see it." With that wisdom from a wise woman I bring you *The Gratitude Attitude…Life Lessons from the Field.* Thanks, Mom.[1]

---

[1] My Mother's last words were "Life is how you see it." She said this while my sister Phil and I were listening to Dr. Wayne Dyer's 101 Affirmations to transform your Life in her hospital room. I know she wanted to let me know that she heard what we were listening to and understood what he was saying.

INTRODUCTION

This book is divided into four sections:

Part I Finding Gratitude is where I share what gratitude is and how finding gratitude transformed my life. Finding gratitude is not as hard as you might think. When some people hear the word "gratitude" they think back to when they were growing up and remember being told they should be grateful—for the meal they couldn't finish or the hand-me-down coat they didn't want to wear. In that context, being grateful seems to mean settling for less. But real gratitude is about opening up your life, creating more joy, and attracting positive experiences and people.

Once you find it, gratitude becomes an attitude, a way of life. Gratitude is a form of appreciation that continues to grow until you no longer recognize your old life. Yes, it can change you that much. Finding gratitude can bring you peace and help you develop humility. When you're practising gratitude, people may even tell you that you seem nicer and look brighter. It can even put a bounce in your step. Yes, gratitude can do all that and more.

Part II Life Lessons from the Field shares with you the life lessons my students learned while partaking in a Leadership Assignment. The stories as told by the students will clearly show you how gratitude becomes a give and receive scenario.

Part III Forever in Gratitude gives you a formula for creating the Gratitude Attitude and keeping it. I also share with you one final life lesson.

Part IV Life Lessons Journal provides you with a list of questions to help you go within and explore the topics discussed in this book. For those of you who wish to print a copy from my website please go to **www.sheilatrask.com.**

GRATITUDE AS A TRANSFORMER

If you want to transform your life, begin each day with the practise of gratitude. As soon as you open your eyes in the morning say thank you. I say, "Thank you for another day, another opportunity to get it right." I then set my intention for the day. It might be something as simple as today I will only eat foods that are good for my body. Then I do what Sandra Gallagher, of the Proctor Gallagher Institute, calls "gratituding," which is the act of writing down at least ten things you are grateful for and more if they keep coming to you; and they will, once you turn on the gratitude tap.

According to Deepak Chopra, "The flow of gratitude from the heart is received by nature in the same spirit it is given, and it is returned back to us as grace."[2] That flow will keep on coming if you practise it daily. I see grace as recycled gratitude. I imagine breathing in grace and breathing out gratitude. It seems abstract at first but becomes clearer as you understand how gratitude brings grace and grace creates more gratitude. Gratitude, like a boomerang, returns to you. The flow of grace stays with you as your life becomes more enjoyable.

---

[2] *Manifesting Grace through Gratitude* - Deepak Chopra and Oprah Winfrey 21 Day Meditation Experience, 2015.

Next, Gallagher suggests you consciously "release" people who make you feel uneasy or uncomfortable when they come to mind. This release enables you to let go of any negative energy you may be carrying. Send them positive wishes as you let them go. I picture them in a hot air balloon and I watch them drift away. This is very freeing and allows you to get on with your day with a clear creative mind. Lastly, take five minutes to just be quiet and ask for guidance for the day. Once you've done this, you've completed the act of "gratituding."[3]

Gratitude is a transformer. For several years I listened to Dr. Wayne Dyer talk about transformation in his 101 Ways to Transform Your Life. In this recording Dyer says, "Transforming your life is a very powerful and exciting thing to undertake. Form is the physical form and the boundaries we have in our life and trans is a prefix meaning to go beyond, to go above, to go past." In other words, Dyer is saying that we can move beyond who we are to become who we wish to be. He says it is not difficult: all you have to do is stretch yourself. One easy way to do this, according to Dyer, is to change the thoughts you think and the words you speak. When you start thinking about gratitude you will find yourself not only thinking more positively, but speaking more positively as well. You will be less likely to say harsh words, as they will not be in the realm of your thoughts.

Gratitude transforms your life by introducing you to your life's purpose. When you are thankful and appreciative, and open to what life brings, you will discover new opportunities. When you start to

---

[3] Go to **www.sheilatrask.com** to download a complimentary gratitude pad.

look at life through the lens of gratitude, you will discover your true potential. You will begin to see what you are here to do.

In the summer of 2015, after attending The Matrixx event in Toronto, I came back home to discover that my thinking had changed so dramatically that I was confused about the direction of my life and what I was doing.[4] This event had changed me so much that I feared I wasn't living my life's passion. I had not been feeling well all summer and was not prepared physically or emotionally to go back to work in September when college resumed. At my doctor's suggestion, I decided to take some time off to reduce my stress and heal from the toll that stress had taken on my body.

Sometimes our life's purpose is wrapped up in our sorrows. I started wondering if mine was as well. Through loss—an accident, illness or death of a loved one—we may find meaning in our lives. I have watched many people devote their lives to a cause associated with their grief, pain, or shame. Two of my friends (Tina Davies and Penny Knapp) have lost their sons to suicide. Both these women are strong activists and public speakers, and they act as caregivers to others grieving the loss of a loved one by suicide. The realization that loss could lead to positive transformation was life changing for me. It meant that I could no longer look at my past and feel victimized or sorry for myself. I now think of life as training that prepares us for what we need to know.

---

[4] The Matrixx is a 6-day live event with Bob Proctor of the Proctor Gallagher Institute. It is designed to allow a limited number of people to work directly on their goals, business-building objectives, challenges, and breakthroughs for more effective wealth creation and accumulation. The event only takes place in Toronto, Canada.

We actually call these lessons into our life so that we can learn what we need to learn. We need to be grateful for this.

I began reading and thinking more about my future. In The Shift, Dyer says, "It is my contention that the bigger the purpose we signed up for in life, the bigger and harder the falls we encounter will be." This idea changed everything for me. It helped me understand why my friends ended up being strong advocates for survivors of suicide loss. I now understand that everything that happens in our lives is part of an education, setting us up for what we are supposed to do: find our life purpose. So no matter what life brings, good or bad, be grateful that it has happened. I am not naive enough to say that it will be easy, but one step at a time can change your life forever. I wondered how this applied to me.

When I go back to Stephenville where I grew up, I like to walk along the beach and pick up rocks, as I collect my thoughts. One day I came across a small object that looked like a unique piece of pottery. I wasn't sure what it was but I knew I had to find out. While I'd been walking on the beach I'd been thinking of Dr. Wayne Dyer who had recently passed. I was saddened by his death. I'd learned so much from his books and recordings and now that I was in crisis, I longed to get his advice about my health and career. When I went to St. John's later that month to see my doctor, I took the object I'd found on the beach with me to have it assessed. Someone had told me it looked like part of a dish from colonial times. Since I'd found it in an area where there had once been a settlement called Sandy Point—where my ancestors had lived—I decided to take the object to the museum to see if it had historical value. If so, I planned to donate it their collection.

The curator I needed to see wasn't in, but she called me later that day, asking me to send pictures. I did and she called right away to tell me it was an old transformer. The minute I heard that word I knew that I had received a message from Dr. Wayne Dyer. The message was to transform my life. Follow my passion. Write my books. Help people move forward with their lives. I had recently purchased a license to facilitate the Thinking Into Results Program from the Proctor Gallagher Institute, and now, as a consultant I could use this program to help people move toward their goals. I was excited about the coaching program because I wanted to work with people who really wanted to reach their goals and do great things. I felt this message to "transform" was telling me I had to follow my heart and do what I'd been trying to do for so many years.

What does this have to do with gratitude? When I had this breakthrough, I had been "gratituding" for a month, and I had done a 21 day gratitude meditation with Deepak Chopra and Oprah Winfrey.[5] Things were opening up for me. I was seeing things that I might previously have ignored. I saw the transformer on a beach full of rocks. So much was happening and I couldn't go back. I was transformed forever. Gratitude will do this. It will show you opportunities that you otherwise might have missed. It will allow you to see things in a different light. Move forward. Take a chance. I heard Dr. Dyer's voice in my head. Transform, transform your life.

Gratitude brings out the best in you, giving you a new appreciation for life and everything in it. Remember, no matter how

---

[5] *Manifesting Grace through Gratitude* - Deepak Chopra and Oprah Winfrey 21 Day Meditation Experience, 2015.

low you go, you can always find your way back up. There are so many things in this life to be grateful for; you just have to look around. When you are feeling low and can't seem to find something to be grateful for, shift your focus from what is wrong in your life to what is right. That's what I needed to do. Focus on what is right.

Take a few minutes each day to sit quietly and find the things that you're grateful for. Start with the smallest things in life and you'll be surprised at how your gratitude grows to encompass everything life has to offer. Think about what makes you who you are. Think about the things you love; the things that make you feel great. By doing this consistently, you will gain a whole new perspective. You will be transformed. You will develop the Gratitude Attitude. You won't have to choose gratitude, because gratitude will choose you, and become a way of life.

LIFE LESSONS TERM PROJECT

Leadership I -CS1120 - Winter 2013

Value: 25% (5 % presentation; 10% class participation; 10% journal)

Positive Attitude

Learn to face life's challenges with an EMPOWERED ATTITUDE.

A positive outlook can change your life. When you change how you feel, you change how you view your life, and the best part is that you will see opportunities that you might have previously missed.

Commit to creating a new improved positive attitude, and see how it expands your energy, interests, and abilities. The results will be amazing!

Positive Attitude Presentation, Discussion, and Journal

Once a week, one student will Present a quote to the class and discuss how that quote speaks to him or her. (Two minute speech.) Select a picture to go with your quote and use PowerPoint to present.

Following your presentation, Lead the students in a Class Discussion about the quote.

Students will be given a copy of each presentation to place in their Journal. Write what the quote means to you and include your thoughts about the presentation or the discussion. Use words, sentences, symbols or pictures; whatever speaks to you. To complete each entry, list 5 things you are grateful for (who or what makes you feel good).

Whenever you feel stressed, sad, or not well, read what you have written. Think a positive thought and write it down. (This can be a word, sentence, or symbol.) Try to write positive things in your journal on a daily basis. (This journal is to promote positive thinking and positive energy, so if you need to discard negative thoughts or work through challenges, use a separate journal to do this, but don't submit it.) This project will begin January 23. I will share a quote with you to demonstrate what I would like you to do. If you are unable to present on your designated date, please ensure that you ask someone to switch with you as this assignment will take the entire semester to complete.

Presentation: your grade will be based on your ability to discuss the quote, engage the class in discussion, and get the other students to share their views. Participation includes your cooperation and participation in class discussion. Journals are to be submitted one week following the last presentation.

PART II

- LIFE LESSONS FROM THE FIELD -

"Gratitude unlocks the fullness of life.
It turns what we have into enough, and more.
It turns denial into acceptance, chaos to order,
confusion to clarity.
It can turn a meal into a feast, a house into a home,
a stranger into a friend."

~ Melody Beattie

A WILDFLOWER BY ANY OTHER NAME IS A STUDENT

Have you ever heard someone refer to another as a bad weed? Students, like wildflowers, grow despite harsh environments. Each and every one of them is beautiful and unique. Why would anyone choose to water just one when they all deserve nourishment, knowledge, love, and attention to help them blossom. Ralph Waldo Emerson asked and answered, "What is a weed? A plant whose virtues have not yet been discovered." And that, dear friends, is what made me think that students are like wildflowers.

Some wildflowers are referred to as weeds, but beauty is always in the eye of the beholder. I prefer wildflowers to cultivated plants as they are natural survivors who grow despite sometimes harsh conditions. You will notice that I use the names of Newfoundland wildflowers in this book to protect the identity of the students. The name of each wildflower is only used once and is not attached to any particular student. The work is not presented as submitted; I have used bits and pieces of the students' work throughout the book, wherever the seeds of wisdom were most likely to bloom.[6]

---

[6] Some of the journal entries have been edited to allow the book to flow. The intent is to create consistency, to expand on some of the thoughts and ideas, and to ensure confidentiality.

This collection of lessons is like a bouquet of wildflowers. They are in my hands, spreading out everywhere, just waiting to be picked.

I present to you my bouquet of wildflowers: Kindra Blake, Amy Callahan, Nicole Collins, Jasmine Collis, Zachary Collis, Kimm Duffney, Linda Flight, Marlena Flynn, Chelsey Hollett, Wendy Piercey, Daniel Power, Geena Rideout, Bailee Shiner, Shelby Welch.

Great job Wildflowers, you are all awesome!

You are the stars who shine brightly, the Graduates of 2014 of the Community Studies Program at the College of the North Atlantic at Grand Falls-Windsor Campus.

With Gratitude,

Sheila
Teacher

LIFE LESSONS JOURNAL

To get the maximum benefit from this book I have provided you with some tools to help guide you. If you go to my website, (www.sheilatrask.com), you will find the following resources: a Life Lessons Journal; a Gratitude Pad; and a guided Gratitude Meditation. You can print off the journal and pad for your convenience.

For your convenience, at the end of this book, I also include the list of questions for each lesson that is included in the online Life Lesson Journal. I invite you to use your Life Lessons Journal to record your reflections on what you have read. Think about the questions I've given you, and write yourself into a new way of thinking. You will be amazed at how quickly you will develop the Gratitude Attitude and start counting the blessings in your life.

You can download The Gratitude Pad to be used each morning as part of your 'gratituding' practice. And if you wish to learn to meditate, you can download a guided Gratitude Meditation recorded by Judith Royle of The Royle Treatment Wellness Centre.[7] Judith does powerful guided meditations using crystal bowls. If you listen to this meditation every morning and again at night before going to

---

[7] To learn more about Judith Royle, her amazing meditations, and her trainings, please go to (www.royletreatmentwellness.com) and/or (www.soulgenesis.com).

sleep, you will discover that gratitude finds you. You will begin to see greatness in places you never knew existed, and, most importantly, you will learn to love yourself and your life. Don't be surprised if others begin to notice changes in you too.

Now, let's get started. Walk with me through this field. Let the wildflowers and me take you on a journey of life lessons.

There are many things to be grateful for. Here are a few to get you started:

- The sound of the ocean
- Rainy days, so you can read a book or do those chores you have been putting off
- Pets who welcome you at the door when you come home
- The smell of clean clothes fresh off the clothes line
- The warm wind brushing your cheek and blowing your hair
- The quiet… so you can collect your thoughts
- The sound of a baby's laughter.

- LESSON ONE -

TALK ABOUT YOUR JOYS

"Talking about our problems is our greatest addiction. Break the habit. Talk about your joys."

~ Rita Schiano

This lesson was the first class presentation for the Life Lessons Project. I introduced the above quote to my students and presented my views on it to demonstrate how I wanted them to approach their assignment. As a visual aid, I used a photo taken by Deanna Bruce, a friend from Stephenville. It shows light shining through the branches of a tree. When I first saw the photo, I asked my friend to tell me the story behind it. She told me she often took a friend's autistic child for a walk, and each time he stopped in the same spot and looked up. One day she took a picture to see what he was looking at. To her surprise it was a street light shining through the branches of the tree. You'd only notice it if you looked up. It reminded me that if you talk about your problems all the time, you're less likely to look up and notice the beauty that is shining through in your life. It also reminded me that when we're talking, we should look up to see the effect our words are having on our listeners.

SHEILA TRASK

How many times have you changed the mood of a friend or family member just by choosing to discuss your problems? I have been guilty of this many times. It was almost as if I thought people needed to know how bad things were. We need to think before we speak! Do we really want to negatively impact the moods of others? Do we really think it helps us or anyone else? Gratitude can help us break the habit of talking about our problems, robbing us of our joy.

How you perceive your problems will change how you address them. When you perceive problems as challenges, you welcome them as opportunities to grow. Challenges make life interesting and overcoming them gives your life meaning. Being grateful will turn your problems into opportunities and your struggles into growth. Finding meaning in life is what gratitude is all about. A new perspective changes everything.[8]

Feeling grateful for whatever life brings accelerates our learning process. Once we have a gratitude attitude, we understand that we have choices regarding our behaviour. It becomes easier to make better decisions. Making better decisions creates more joy in our lives.

Sometimes, we develop habits as a way of dealing with our emotions. We may choose to bury or suppress our emotions by over-eating, smoking, drinking, gambling, judging others, or saying negative things. This is an effort to ignore how we really feel. All of

---

[8] One of the first things I teach students when they enter my program is that if they think of their problems as challenges, those challenges will become their inspiration to go on to greater things. Once students begin to view problems as challenges, they learn that anything is possible. My students will be the first to say that this new way of thinking has helped get them through many crises in their lives.

these behaviours are just numbing the pain and keeping the emotions buried. Some people are even addicted to being sad. This explains why they talk negatively. They can't wait to share their problems with others because unconsciously they need to feel sad. Dr. Dyer, in You'll See It When You Believe It, says, "Sadness is an attitude that is habituated over a lifetime of focusing on what is wrong and missing in our lives." If an attitude of sadness can become a habit, then joy can become a habit as well.

Challenge yourself! The next time you are about to discuss your problems, STOP! Talk about your joys instead; what great thing happened to you or your friend or your child? Look for joy in the world by looking for the things you are grateful for, and bring joy to the world by sharing it. Dr. Wayne Dyer says "Finding joy means consciously deciding to process your life in ways that focus on gratefulness for what you have." We can start this process by paying attention to our words, what we say to other people. Think about it: what do you talk about when you see other people?

Now, let's hear some words of wisdom from a variety of Wildflowers. They are in no particular order, and the type of wildflower chosen for each has no particular meaning. It merely preserves the identity of the student... from the field.....**Teacher**

LIFE LESSONS
FROM THE WILDFLOWERS

Dog Violet

This quote helped me realize that talking negatively is a big addiction of mine. I seem to dwell on my problems instead of thinking about the wonderful things and people in my life. So how do I get rid of that bad habit? Well, every day I will remind myself of all the great people I know and think about the good things that are happening around me. Being happy and grateful for the good in our lives allows us to move forward towards the goals we set for ourselves. I am going to focus on my goals. Five times a day I will say, "I am so blessed and thankful."

I am grateful for…

- My family, especially my children
- All the friends I have met in this journey I call life
- Having joy… it is awesome!
- My boy making his bed
- Reruns of "Three's Company" as it makes me laugh

Golden Tickseed

Although I may not always talk about my problems, I do talk about myself a lot. I go on and on about something that no one may even care about. But I can relate to how listening to someone complain about their problems all the time can become very tiring. It might be better to discuss your problem with a friend and try to find a solution. But going around just talking about your problems... well, that is just another problem.

I am grateful for...

- A supportive family
- Believing in myself
- A good sense of humour
- Living in a safe town
- Having a healthy home to live in

Cornflower

This was a big eye opener for me and for a lot of other people in the class. Who wants to run into a person who gripes about his/her problems all the time? Also, I don't want to be that person. I'm going to commit to thinking of at least one positive thing to say every day, even if it is just a comment about the sun coming out for ten minutes or the dog wagging her tail when I come home. That is really what makes life worthwhile, getting that Gratitude Attitude.

I am grateful for...

- My friends
- Clean air

- Sunshine
- Sand on the beach
- My dog

Celandine

If we can perceive our problems as opportunities, our battles are already half won. If we look for the joyful things in our life, we will have more to be grateful for and more positive things to talk about. Sometimes I still have the tendency to focus on my chronic pain, personal issues left over from my childhood, and my procrastination. I could use the energy that I pour into talking about my problems to solve them instead. To change this habit, I will devote my energy to looking at things more positively. That will empower me to have more constructive thoughts and ideas. They say it takes twenty-one days to form a habit or make something a routine. I guess that means I better get started! Here comes the Gratitude Attitude.

I am grateful for...

- A roof over my head and a place to sleep at night
- My friends and family
- Keeping myself in a state of positive mental health
- Passing my courses and doing well in school
- The ability to express myself in writing

African Daisy

Until I heard this quote, it had never occurred to me that talking about problems could become a habit. I feel that I don't talk about my problems too much, but I know people who do. This brings down their mood and also affects everyone else around them. Some people may enjoy receiving pity from others by portraying themselves as a victim, but this doesn't really help them in the long run. We must empower ourselves and the people around us. A positive attitude is contagious.

I used to feel that talking about my joys, or telling a "good news story" would appear boastful, so I always avoided it. After thinking about this quote I realized it may not be bragging at all. Maybe my good news and positive attitude will bring a smile to someone else's face, or better yet, remind them of their own good news.

Addictions can have a negative or (in some cases) a positive influence on our lives. Choose positive. One of my addictions is music. Music brings me great joy, happiness, and comfort. I am thankful for uplifting lyrics that brighten my day.

Even though there may be darkness around us, if we are able to see the light, it will increase. I have decided to make a conscious effort to talk about my joys, to inspire my family and friends to talk about the good things in their lives. There are so many things in life for us to be thankful for, so why waste time pointing out the negative. This is the beginning of a more positive attitude for me. From now on I am going to talk about my joys. I am going to have a Gratitude Attitude.

I am grateful for...

- My mother. Without her I would not be the person I am today. She has taught me what it means to be strong and resilient. She has shown me unconditional love even when I have been hard to love. I am so proud of the relationship we have today.

- The memories I have of my father. Although I lost him at a young age, I am thankful I had him in my life. I am thankful that I had the love of my father. The memories of him are something that gives me comfort.

- Music, because it brings me joy.

- Healthy lifestyle changes. Since I have been exercising and eating healthier, my self-confidence has grown.

- The opportunity to be a student. For the first time in my life I feel like I am exactly where I am supposed to be, which is such an amazing feeling. This week has taught me that regardless of the situation, there is always light.

Yellow Rattle

I hope to influence others to adopt this new Gratitude Attitude so that it will improve their lives as well. I find it refreshing and self-motivating to have the confidence to think positively about myself and others.

Since hearing this quote, I started to notice when I was focusing on the more negative aspects of my life. I began paying attention to discussions among my family and friends. I was amazed when I started to catch myself talking about negative things too. I came to the realization that I needed to transform my thinking to focus on the more positive things in my life. Lord knows, I have much to be thankful for. I have found that the more I look for positive things to talk about, the easier it becomes to be positive. Practise, practise, practise.

I am grateful for…

- A loving relationship
- People who believe in me
- Great friends
- Memories of my Nan's laughter
- My chance in life to come as far as I have

Teacher

Whether or not we dwell on the past, engage in negative conversation, or give in to disappointment, it is all within our control. These behaviours contribute to negative thinking and have a negative impact on our minds and bodies. Be mindful: observe your own thoughts and be aware of what you're saying to others. Remember, you have the power to lift someone's spirits or bring them down, just through a simple conversation. If someone else is talking to you in a negative manner, change the subject or excuse yourself from the conversation. Of course, there may be times when you need to seek someone's advice about a problem or someone may need to seek your advice. That's different. But if people are complaining just for the sake of complaining, no one benefits.

By talking about your joys, you will create a positive atmosphere, encouraging others to do the same. If you make these changes in your life, you will find that you will be happier, more grateful, and more joyful. Take it one step at a time; one conversation at a time.

Challenge Yourself

Try this little experiment for one week and see how easily you can change the tone of a conversation. Pay attention to what's being said.

If someone starts talking about their problems, see if you can bring the conversation around to a more positive tone. If you keep track of your conversations, you will begin to see patterns of behaviour. Who do you talk to about your problems? Why do you think that is? Notice who tried to talk to you about their problems. What does this mean to you? If you had the opportunity to change the subject, how did that go? How did the person react? What feelings did you experience? How did you feel physically? An example is, "I had butterflies in my stomach." Keep these thoughts in mind when you're writing in your Life Lessons Journal.

Life Lessons Journal

Please go to **Part IV Life Lessons Journal** at the end of the book to complete the questions on this life lesson or go to **www.sheilatrask.com** to print off your own journal.

- LESSON TWO -

RISE FROM THE GROUND

LIKE A SKYSCRAPER

"Go on and try to tear me down.
I will be rising from the ground like a skyscraper..."

~ Demi Lovato

This first student presentation is by a wildflower I'll call Pitcher Plant. Negative self-talk eroded Pitcher Plant's confidence and lowered her self-esteem. When she realized how negative thinking was destroying her sense of self-worth and perpetuating her eating disorder, she decided it had to stop. Replacing negativity with gratitude changed the way she saw herself and helped her conquer her disorder. The quote she chose reflects her fight to combat negative self-talk. In her recovery, she found herself rising from the ground like a skyscraper.

Pitcher Plant

These lyrics inspire me. They make me feel invincible and stronger. I wish that I'd had a role model when I was young. It would have allowed me to focus on who I wanted to be when I grew up and what it would take to be that sort of person. I would have felt the strength back then that I do today when I read those lyrics. Having a role model can be beneficial.[9] I think it would have made me feel okay about being myself, and if I appeared different than other teens that would have been okay too. A role model may have allowed me to accept myself more and that would have meant better self-esteem. Who knows, I may have avoided my eating disorder. I can't go back and change the past but I can learn from my previous mistakes.

When I was young, I dwelled on negative comments. If someone said "you can't" then I thought "I can't." Hearing those words kept me from doing what I really wanted to do. The words controlled my life and the decisions I made. I dwelled on them so much that I started to believe them. I started to feel that I wasn't good enough and that I would never fulfill my dreams. I stopped believing in myself. I kept repeating negative words inside my head. I think when we believe negative things about ourselves, we are less likely to try to reach our goals. We may find it easier to just run away. I stopped eating.

One day I made a decision: starting today, I am going to stand up to any negative thoughts or unkind words from others and, more importantly, from myself. There will be no room for them because I will fill my head with so many thoughts of gratefulness and positivity that I will be beaming from ear to ear. If I even think that someone is

---

[9] I recommend you read Danielle Joworski's, *The Athena Prodigies: Empowering Women Empowering Girls.*

THE GRATITUDE ATTITUDE | 51

trying to tear me down, I will feel inspired to rise above them.

When I began recovery I started looking past fear and self-doubt. I started trusting myself and my abilities. I stopped listening to the negative self-talk. I started looking at all the good things in my life. Once I started doing that, I began to see inspiration all around me. It came in many forms (people, animals, nature). I draw strength and determination from knowing that other people struggle too and they might need my encouragement. I discovered that I'm the only one who can bring me down and hold me back. It is my self-worth and determination that prevents me from falling.

I want to help others who are struggling with their self-esteem to learn to appreciate the good things in their lives, to find the courage to do anything they want to do, to be anything they want to be. I want to help children overcome any challenges they may have with self-esteem. I want them to know that if someone puts them down and they feel less, they need to remember to rise back up like a skyscraper. Be the best that you can be; that is what counts. Each child is unique and special in his/her own way.

Teacher

Self-esteem is one of the most important issues in the lives of children, teens, and even adults. People with good self-esteem are generally happier, healthier, and enjoy life more than those with low self-esteem. Everyday life can make us feel vulnerable so raising our self-esteem is something we need to work on, on a daily basis.

To grow your self-esteem you need to learn to love yourself. You need to commit to doing things that will make you feel good about yourself. One way to do this is by setting challenging, yet realistic goals. The more goals you set, the more goals you accomplish, the better you feel, the higher your self-esteem climbs. When you feel good about yourself, you will be less likely to do things that will harm your mind or your body. The great part about this is that the high you get from success is far better than any artificial high you will get from drugs or alcohol. Another way to boost your self-esteem is by cultivating the gratitude attitude. As you start to appreciate your abilities and the good things in your life, you will start to think about yourself in a more positive light. You will be good to yourself and to others and your life will change. The better you feel about yourself, the less vulnerable you will be to negative comments or criticism. You will stop worrying about what others are saying or thinking about you.

Let's hear what the other wildflowers have to say about rising up from the ground like a skyscraper.

LIFE LESSONS

FROM THE WILDFLOWERS

Pink Lady's Slipper

This quote helped me realize that talking negatively is a big addiction of mine. I seem to dwell on my problems instead of thinking about the wonderful things and people in my life. So how do I get rid of that bad habit? Well, every day I will remind myself of all the great people I know and think about the good things that are happening around me. Being happy and grateful for the good in our lives allows us to move forward towards the goals we set for ourselves. I am going to focus on my goals. Five times a day I will say, "I am so blessed and thankful."

When I think about this quote, I feel fearless determination, and it inspires me to face life's challenges head on. If I have that kind of attitude, I can accomplish anything. This reminds me of my childhood when many of my peers tormented and bullied me. Although it was a difficult time, today I thank those people because they taught me that I'm responsible for my own feelings. No one can make me feel bad or not good enough without my permission. I still struggle with self-confidence, but I am learning that it is my responsibility to love myself. No matter how great the challenge, we must try to be resilient, positive, and overcome hardships. I'm increasing my confidence by working out at the gym. When I see the results I am getting I feel better about myself. I realize that at school or work, or anything I do in life, hard-work and determination will bring about results and results will increase confidence. I have learned to love myself, and that has done wonders for me. I now have a Gratitude Attitude.

I am grateful for...

- My two pet cats, sisters I adopted from the SPCA two years ago. They each have their own distinct personalities and provide great comfort and companionship, especially when I'm feeling alone.

- My health. So many people have challenges, disabilities, and health issues. I am so grateful that I am not living with any of these obstacles.

- My classmates and instructor. The atmosphere is encouraging. I feel as if we are all here for a reason and we each have something different to bring to the table. My school experience thus far has been far greater than I imagined it could be.

Labrador Tea

I think of all the times my ex-husband told me I would never be able to do anything. Everything he told me I couldn't do, I have done, tenfold. The more he said I couldn't, the harder I tried. I grew stronger and more motivated. Being grateful for what you have encourages you to ignore negative talk, whether it is coming from you or someone else; all you hear then is encouragement and applause. I will always be grateful for the encouragement I got from my friends and family to do the things I was told were impossible. Just like Audrey Hepburn said, "Impossible says I'm possible!"

I am grateful for...

- Someone to love and to be loved by him in return
- The sweet times I had with my dear Mother
- Yellow roses... my favorite flower
- The opportunity to share my positive attitude with my friends
- My sports car because it helped me do things that I was told were impossible for me to do

Soapwort

In grade twelve I had a lot of trouble with math. It made me feel stupid. My parents told me the only reason I couldn't understand it was because I had convinced myself that I couldn't. I got a great tutor and I passed with a 70. I was so proud of myself. I remember the day my grades came in the mail. My mother and I were holding our breath when we opened the envelope. We screamed with glee when we saw my mark. Since then, I will always say "I can" because I have learned that first and foremost, I have to believe in myself. This quote reminds me of how I talked myself into thinking I couldn't do math. Once I got beyond that way of thinking I was successful. Once you stop beating yourself up, you will find that what used to challenge you is now much easier to do. It is like blockages start to tumble down. I am so grateful that I realized this before it was too late.

I am grateful for…

- My parents pushing me on
- A great tutor
- Believing in myself
- Not dwelling on the negatives
- Overcoming obstacles in my life

Alphalpha

We can walk into a crowded room where every single person is laughing at us and talking about us, but unless we allow that negativity to affect us, it can't. We usually blame others for making us feel a certain way. I have blamed others for things I didn't like about myself only to realize that I chose to be that way. We all have choices in life. When I was younger, I had a friend who used to put me down, and I would feel bad. I would repeat those negative words over and over in my head. I let that abuse continue for years and hated myself for it until I realized I was better than that. I needed to look at what was good in my life and be grateful for it. So I walked out of her life and started fresh. Starting over is scary but doable. Making the choice to leave an unhealthy relationship is the first step. Someone else can't bring you down unless you allow them to. Choose supportive and loving friendships. You will be grateful.

I am grateful for…

- Clothes
- Hot baths
- My dog
- My friends

- The quiet

Teacher

Our self-esteem can be fragile so we need to cultivate it by learning to love ourselves. You cannot love others if you do not love yourself. Everything begins with you. Feeling good about yourself is about allowing yourself to be the best you can be, keeping your head up, looking straight ahead, and never looking back. The past doesn't matter. What matters is that you are here now, in the present, learning to love yourself. We all feel fragile at some point in our lives; however, our self-esteem gets a boost when we find gratitude. It is hard to feel bad about yourself when you are grateful for everything life has to offer.

Pleasant memories can boost our self-esteem. I remember two special women who helped cultivate my self-esteem: one by feeding my love of books, the other by encouraging me to write.

As a four-year-old child, I was allowed to get my own library card. Prior to that, I had to depend on my sisters to get me books. I remember going to the library on a daily basis, feeling all grown up and independent with my own library card. Sometimes the librarian, Mrs. White, used to let me help out. It was a small building but it was filled to the brim with books. They used cards to file away books and to keep track of borrowers. I would stay as late as she would let me. I was so grateful for her kindness. Every day I took home the maximum four books I was allowed, read them all, and returned them the next day to get four more. My love of books was encouraged and for this I am grateful.

When I was in Grade 7, my English teacher, Mary MacDonald, encouraged my love of writing. She would get us to write a story in class at least a couple of times a week. She encouraged me to continue writing because I loved it, and her encouragement allowed my creativity to flow. Writing those stories was the one thing I could do to make me feel really good about myself. I used an exercise book and sometimes I wrote a story every day just because I liked doing it and I loved to see her reaction. She taught me to do what I love and encouraged me to follow my passion. When she passed I felt so sad and I thought about how good she had made me feel. Helping kids develop what they love to do does wonders for their self-esteem. To let you in on a little secret, I still like to write in exercise books.

When we use gratitude to open ourselves up to do what we love, we awaken joy and beauty all around us; perhaps it was there all along but we just didn't see it. Our life becomes easier, more fun, and more meaningful when we are grateful.

Challenge Yourself

Do something that makes you feel good. Write in your journal about what you did and how it made you feel. Doing things for others can boost your self-esteem. Give it a try.

Life Lessons Journal

Please go to **Part IV Life Lessons Journal** at the end of the book to complete the questions on this life lesson or go to **www.sheilatrask.com** to print off your own journal.

- LESSON THREE -

WORRY CAUSES FEAR

CAUSES WORRY

"We are, perhaps, uniquely among the earth's creatures, the worrying animal. We worry away our lives."

~ **Lewis Thomas,** *The Medusa and the Snail*

"The only thing we have to fear is fear itself."

~ Franklin D. Roosevelt

Because worry causes fear, and fear causes worry, I decided to combine the presentations of these two quotes into one lesson.

Worrying is a habit. It's difficult to overcome and it can have devastating effects. Simply put, worrying is a waste of your time. It eats up your energy, keeping you from doing things that you enjoy. It's putting your focus on something you don't want to happen. Yet most of the things we worry about never happen. So why do people worry? I think worry is instilled in us at a young age. As we incorporate the tendency to worry into our personalities we may begin to fear more and more things.

I believe we are born fearless but the constant scolding from concerned parents, siblings, and well-meaning adults teaches us fear. "Stop that you will hurt yourself." "You can't do that you might get in trouble." "Don't do that, it is not ladylike." These constant messages make us fearful of trying new things because we might hurt ourselves, or we might get in trouble, or others might not like us. It is easy to see how children begin to worry. In many ways worry is fear, fear of what might happen.

Fear is a learned behavior and anything that is learned can be unlearned. We can unlearn fear by standing up for ourselves, by not caring what others think, by going after what we desire in life, and by following our dreams. When we have faith in ourselves we know that fear has no place in our lives. Think about it: if inventors had not been fearless, we would not have the many things we enjoy in this modern world. We have nothing to fear: not failure or success.

Ground Ivy is a young mother and, like all mothers, she worries obsessively about her child. When worry becomes fear, it can interfere with a child's natural upbringing. If a parent is fearful, he or she may deprive the child of many valuable experiences, such as having fun trying new things, learning to cope with challenging situations, and dealing with disappointment. In Ground Ivy's presentation, she shared her strategy of replacing worry with gratitude.

Ground Ivy

I have learned to live in the moment and appreciate every day. This is not something that comes naturally to me so I have to constantly work on it. I've always worried about everything and anything. Looking back, I can't remember what I've stressed myself out about. I am sure it hasn't been anything worth the energy.

When I was pregnant, my tendency to worry was taken to new extremes. I imagined every struggle and every bridge that my child would have to face in his lifetime. It made me fearful. When he was born and I realized how much I loved him, it became even worse. It took a few months to realize that there is no point in worrying about whether he will able to maintain healthy eating habits as a child or smoke as a teenager. The concern is still there, but I have chosen to focus on the age he is right now. Staying in the present has allowed me to stop being fearful of something that has not happened. Now I am able to appreciate and be grateful for every moment I share with my son. I realized that worrying will take away from the great possibilities and joys of today. My gratitude for having my son in my life is far greater than wasting my time worrying. I think we should take everything that today has to offer, and choose to not let fear overcome our thoughts.

I am grateful for ...

- My son
- Being a mother
- Learning to live in the present
- Gratitude and the power it has given me

SHEILA TRASK

Teacher

Being grateful for what we have eradicates fear, as one student demonstrated to me on a regular basis. Mountain Bluet truly was a wildflower in many ways. He once told me fear didn't frighten him. He made us laugh and shake our heads, and he skillfully brought the students together as a group. I learned a lot from this wildflower. He wasn't always sure why he was there, but he never missed a day of class. He saw things at a level that most students couldn't comprehend. His talents were unique. It seemed only fitting that he would use a quote about fear, as if I had to choose one word to describe him I would use fearless. This wildflower came to life when he gave his presentation.

Mountain Bluet

This quote reminds me of what I was told when I was learning to drive: you must look away from transport trucks coming towards you on the highway or your car will follow the path to the truck. To stay safe, we must stay on our own side of the road. The same can be said about life. We need to stay on our own path, as it is a safer and much surer route to our own happiness. If we think we have to be like everyone else because we are afraid to be ourselves, we will be the car heading into the path of the truck. Forget what others are saying or wearing or how they do things. Do your own thing. Be your own person.

Don't let fear make you one of the crowd, for it will rob you of your uniqueness. It may feel safer to follow others, but that is fear talking. Be yourself and you will be safe.

I am grateful for...

- My life and happiness
- My safety
- The upbringing that my parents gave me
- Being born in Newfoundland
- Transportation

Teacher

We waste our time thinking about the future and all the bad things that might happen. What is the point? We waste away our life with worry. Worrying takes away the joy of today. When you look at it from a biological perspective, all animals are the same. They eat, breathe, and live. A bird does not spend its day worrying and being afraid about what will happen when winter comes. It enjoys the warmth of the day, and knows when the time is right it will be ready to migrate. If we teach ourselves to focus on the present we will be less likely to worry about the future. We will get rid of the negative "what ifs." We will focus on the here and now and the beauty of the moment.

Now let's hear what the worrying wildflowers did to combat their tendency to worry and be fearful.

LIFE LESSONS
FROM THE WILDFLOWERS

Threetooth Cinquefoil

I too am a creature of worry. I worry over anything and everything. How will I pay the bills? Will I lose my friends? Will today be a good day?

For the last three years, my son has been my main source of stress and concern. I started to worry about him the moment I found out I was pregnant. My thoughts were consumed with questions and concerns. Will I be a good mom? Am I eating enough?

While I was pregnant I made all of the decisions for my baby or at least that's how it felt. When he was tucked away safely inside of me, I was in control. But the moment he took his first breath, I felt my fear of the dangers of the world rushing in. Immediately, I started worrying. What if I lose him? What if he gets sick? What would I do? I was so afraid. I started questioning everything I did and didn't do. If something happened to him how would I cope?

Sometimes when someone means so much to us, we pull away from them out of fear of losing them. I didn't want to do that with my son. I have felt that fear every day since he came into my life. If anything happened to him my life would be shattered. Slowly, I have been trying to alter the part of me that lives in fear by allowing other loved ones into my life. I am grateful for them.

To fully enjoy life, I can't live in fear and spend my time worrying over everything that might happen. I know I will never be totally free of fear and worry but I have accepted this as a normal part of life, and I try not be consumed by it. I know that in order to enjoy my son, I have to allow him to live and experience the world. This can't happen if I live in fear or spend too much time worrying. As a parent, I have to teach my son to be happy and carefree, to enjoy life and appreciate it. I have to model this behaviour for him. This is the only way we can have an amazing mother and son relationship. I am grateful for my son and the opportunity to be his mother.

I am grateful for…

- Wild animals that are free of zoos
- Airplanes that take us to visit cities worldwide
- Culture
- Dancing
- Singing even if I can't hit a note

Shrubby Cinquefoil

I spend way too much time worrying. I worry about what it would mean if I didn't complete my education. I worry about the consequences of my procrastination. I worry about conversations I may never have with anyone. I worry about my weight and my looks and whether or not I will be good enough for that special person I hope to find. I worry my life away just as the quote suggests.

I guess the answer is to develop strategies and practices that build my self-confidence and allow me to live in the present. Too often I think that I am lazy, useless, and not trying my best to become successful. These thoughts need to be replaced with the realization that I am trying the best I can. I need to be grateful for what I am able to do.

Sometimes we allow our fear to defeat us. Just as I am in control of letting fear and doubts govern my thoughts and actions, I am also in control of overcoming them and replacing them with positive and productive thoughts. I am slowly getting there. I think that realization is half the battle.

So today I am going to start a gratitude attitude. Being grateful for what I have should help me reduce my anxiety about everything. The self-love I deserve will come much easier if I am in a state of gratitude. I don't know why I haven't thought of this before. This project has really opened my eyes to the importance of being grateful. I will make it a permanent part of my life. I am confident it will shift my thinking.

I learned from Teacher that getting help is a sign of strength. It is important to know when you need help. There is no shame in getting help. We give it all the time, but we are hesitant to receive it. It is like we feel less if we need help. It is just as important to be able to receive help as to give it. This is a lesson that all caregivers—paid or not—need to learn. Worrying uses up precious time that we could be using for something meaningful in our lives. "Thanks, Teacher."

THE GRATITUDE ATTITUDE | 67

I am grateful for...

- Skipping rocks at the beach
- My grandmother's macaroni and cheese
- Naps on a lazy Sunday afternoon
- The joy that I get from the humour in Calvin and Hobbes
- The smell of freshly mowed grass

Blueberry

Fear is a mind killer. It limits our potential. Most of our challenges are fear based and self-created. Our fears can create barriers to happiness and success. But if we try, we can control our fears and not let them stifle us.

When we fear that we can't do something right we put things off. Procrastination for me is based on fear, a fear of success and the world that exists outside my comfort zone. If I remain fixated on my fears I will miss much of what this world has to offer in the way of knowledge, experience, and physical, mental, and spiritual pleasures.

Gratitude helps me achieve freedom in many ways. I feel very fortunate to have been blessed with all that a person could want in terms of family and friends. Their encouragement helps override my fears. If we can rid ourselves of our fears, we can achieve incredible things. Fear makes us doubt ourselves. Gratitude gives us self-love and confidence. Once we eliminate self-doubt, the sky is the limit. Always be grateful!

I am grateful for…

- People who support me
- Friendship
- Sunsets
- Having a barbecue with family
- Reading poetry of the "greats"
- Riding my bike
- Time spent in meditation and contemplation

Blue Eyed Grass

We surround ourselves with walls to try to cope with our fears. Fear can control our lives if we let it. Understanding helps us face our fears. For example, many kids are afraid of the dark, and it controls them every time they go to bed. As we grow older we realize that a dark room is nothing to fear. But when we are young, the fear is real.

Fear is just a feeling, and like all other feelings, we can control it. For a lot of people, fear is probably one of the toughest feelings to control. There is only one thing to do: face fear by looking at the other side of fear. Fear is usually illogical. When I realize that what I am afraid of is not real, then I focus on something more pleasing. This helps me move past fear and on to something else, something more positive like my daughter, who continues to amaze me with her accomplishments. I am grateful that I can be a positive influence in her life; this inspires me to live and let go.

I am grateful for…

- People who inspire me
- All the mistakes I have made and how they have taught me valuable lessons in life
- A vehicle that gets me to school every day
- Radios that play beautiful music

Bottle Brush

I am afraid of pretty much everything: people, the dark, new things, and the unknown. I have been working on this for a long time. I have learned that it is a mind over matter challenge. But I believe that we need to have some fear in us. We need this fear because without it, we would think that we are invincible. This could be dangerous. I think fear can keep us out of trouble. So fear is not really good or bad, it just is. The trick is to figure out how to get it on your side.

One of my biggest fears was losing my parents. I realized one day that if I spent all my time obsessing about losing my parents, I would not be able to enjoy them while they are here. I think that was a turning point for me. I began to look at fear in a completely different light. I started looking at fear for what it is—a feeling that is not real if we don't let it be. I began spending my time being grateful for my parents. This allowed to me to spend quality time with them and enjoy them.

SHEILA TRASK

I am grateful for…

- Fear
- Looking straight through the eye of a needle
- Not driving into the arch… yet
- Friends and family that push me on

Oysterleaf

Fear makes me think about procrastination. I could be just making excuses or rationalizing when I say this, but it frustrates me when people tell me to "just get it done." They have no idea how much I fear getting things done or, really, not getting things done at all. I've searched for an answer, but I don't know whether it is fear, anxiety, or depression that makes me put my life on hold. Whatever it is that prevents me from contributing to my own success is not as simple as laziness or a way of thinking. I read somewhere that some people would rather be viewed as lazy than as stupid. They fear not being right, not being perfect, of being thought of as anything less than brilliant. This makes them procrastinate. Fear and procrastination are partners in crime. They hold you back. Once you understand this, you can tackle them head on. Be grateful for your abilities. Gratitude will give you strength to do things now not later.

I am grateful for…

- Working towards a career as a healer of sorts
- The sun in the morning and the moon at night
- Decaf coffee
- A roaring fireplace
- Sushi

- Toutons[10]

Downy Cinquefoil

I am a big worrier or at least I was. I have to say that the last few weeks have not been so worrisome. I have learned to take it day by day, appreciate what I have, and not worry about what I can't change. The things that have happened are in the past so there is no point in worrying about them. I can't change them. I am improving my life so I look forward to the future. I will not worry about the everyday stuff. My goal is to enjoy what I have and be grateful for everything in my life. Now I am a warrior not a worrier.

I am grateful for...

- The morning sun
- The evening breeze
- The dog sleeping on my bed
- The quiet of the night

Teacher

As an Educator I have come to realize how much students tend to worry and how this worry can turn into anxiety. Students who procrastinate are some of the worst worriers. The procrastination seems to enhance the worrying and the worrying seems to exacerbate the procrastination. I try to keep an eye on this and help students before they worry themselves into failing. The longer I have taught the better I have become at identifying these students early on and

---

[10] A touton is a Newfoundland delicacy which consists of fried bread dough, cinnamon, and brown sugar. It's eaten with molasses.

helping them develop strategies to reduce their anxiety. Students who tend to be anxious are often "last minute people." They do everything the last minute. They even come to class at the last minute. All of the running and "last minuting" serves to increase their anxiety. Once they recognize the little habits that are not serving them well, they are much better at controlling their anxiety and worry regarding other aspects of their life.

My mother was a worrier. She worried all the time even though I kept telling her that she was wasting her time because most of what she worried about never happened. As every parent knows, it is hard not to worry about our children, regardless of their age, especially when they are away from us. I used to worry about my Mom worrying; that is how habitual and contagious worrying can be. I spent a lot of time talking to my Mom on the phone trying to help relieve her worries over her ten adult children. The worrying only increased as the family grew to include grandchildren and great-grandchildren.

Even though I recognized this trait in my mother, I found myself worrying too. I decided to start changing my thinking. Every time I caught myself worrying, I started counting the things I am grateful for in my life and the good things I expect to happen in the future. This not only keeps my mind occupied, it also plants seeds for the great things I'd like to have happen. Choosing good, positive thoughts is certainly a way to overcome worry. Sometimes we need to make a conscious choice to not worry. Distract yourself by counting your blessings. Being grateful is about appreciating what you have right here, right now.

One of things I am grateful for is the ocean. I love the ocean. I didn't realize that some people were afraid of it until I met a woman from the interior of British Columbia. She told me the ocean really scared her. She didn't know why, but I thought it might have something to do with a fear of the unknown. She had never experienced the ocean as I had.

I grew up near the ocean. My hometown of Stephenville, Newfoundland and Labrador, Canada, is on the Atlantic Ocean. Our school was on a bank overlooking the water. Most days at recess we played in sight of the ocean. It was a backdrop for our everyday lives at home, school, and church. The ocean was all around us so we took it for granted, just like our skin. Even today when I go home I love to stand by the ocean and look it in the eye and say, "Hey, how are you feeling today?" I often imagine that the ocean has feelings. Some days it looks bright and happy, while other days it looks angry. I do not fear the ocean despite the fact that many have lost their lives at sea.

Many people I know go to the ocean to walk along the beach when they're trying to think through a problem, make a decision, or escape their pain, fear, or worry. They take comfort from the sights, sounds, smells, and peacefulness. For those who love it, going to the ocean is like getting a warm hug, an embrace that says everything will be okay.

For me, going to the ocean is a way to wash away the stress and strains of everyday life. The ocean helps me search my soul. I think more clearly when I'm walking on the beach. When I'm thinking through a challenging situation and I come to a resolution, it feels like the water is taking my problems away from me and washing them out to sea. I like this visual. The ocean energizes me. I visualize the waves bringing in joy, bliss, and positive thoughts.

There is healing all around us. We just have to see it. I am so grateful for the ocean. Being grateful leaves no room for fear.

Gratitude can scare fear away. It can make you fearless. All you have to say is, "I am so grateful that I have more power than fear. When I think of all of the great things I have in my life, I feel fearless. When I think of all the great people I have in my life, I feel fearless." If you repeat this over a few times you will feel empowered.

Challenge Yourself

The next time you catch yourself worrying ask yourself; "What is the likelihood that this is going to happen?" Then think of a different outcome, a more positive outcome that makes you smile. Now hold that thought and repeat it in your head.

Life Lessons Journal

Please go to **Part IV Life Lessons Journal** at the end of the book to complete the questions on this life lesson or go to **www.sheilatrask.com** to print off your own journal.

- LESSON FOUR -

YOU HAVE TO LET GO

TO MOVE FORWARD

"Getting over a painful experience is much like crossing the monkey bars. You have to let go at some point in order to move forward."

~ C.S. Lewis

Sometimes you have to let go to move forward. You can't move forward until you understand what is holding you back. Think about emotions such as sadness, anger, anxiety, and worry. Do any of these affect your decisions? Do any of these affect your thoughts or your behaviours? If you are feeling sad all the time, your sadness may come from wanting more. You may want more love, acceptance, reassurance or safety. If you are feeling angry, you may be holding on to something from your past that you need to let go. Anxiety and worry are issues related to the future, whereas sadness and anger are connected to the past. We need to be present. If we stay in the present, our thoughts and feelings about the past and our fears about the future will stop holding us back.

Meadowsweet has been through a lot in her young life. Yet everyday she finds reasons to let go and keep moving forward.

Meadowsweet

My parents divorced when I was eight years old. Not having a father figure has certainly played a role in shaping who I am today.

We grow wiser and more self-aware as we learn from our experiences. I realize that my parents are happier apart, and I can't blame myself for their divorce.

I can't speak for my classmates, but I am at my happiest when I am helping others. Perhaps my coping mechanism for dealing with my own problems is losing myself in the trials and tribulations of my fellow human beings. This may work, but it is not necessarily healthy. I need to realize that my own troubles are just as important as those of other people. Letting go of the past and acknowledging that it is behind me (said and done) is a good way to move forward with my life. It is time for me to live in the present, where I can do the most good for myself and others. I learned from Teacher that it is common to focus on others so we don't have to focus on ourselves. Many caregivers are guilty of this. Today I will be grateful for my life experiences. I will learn from them and then let go, so that as I move forward, I move forward in a healthy way.

I am grateful for...

- Autumn, my favorite season
- Confidants and people who are genuine
- Movie theaters

- That I live in Canada, a country free from war and tyranny
- All of the people around me in a given day
- Rain on the rooftop: the sound gives me the best sleep
- An incredibly warm jacket, when it is freezing cold outdoors
- Seeing someone accomplish their goals
- Playing a board game with friends
- Simply spending time talking with close friends

Teacher

Divorce is a life changing experience for a child. It explains why some children grow up to be sad or angry. But it doesn't have to be this way. Children often feel responsible for their parents' divorce. This is because they are too young to understand that it has nothing to do with them. When they grow up they are able to understand and stop blaming themselves and/or other people, in order to let go and move forward with their lives. It is important to reinforce this message to children so they won't carry guilt over something that was beyond their control. Now let's read how some of the wildflowers let go and moved forward.

LIFE LESSONS
FROM THE WILDFLOWERS

Purple Chokeberry

I can relate many experiences in my life to crossing monkey bars and having to let go to move on. Leaving my ex-husband is one such example. It was a very painful experience. I thought I would never be able to have another relationship because of the way I had been treated. I hated all men and couldn't trust them for a very long time. I was afraid to let go of the cross bars. Then I met the man I am with now. I slowly got to know him and I began to realize that all men are not the same. I let go of the cross bar and I moved forward. For the first time I am truly happy with my life. I have a lot to be grateful for.

I am grateful for...

- The people in my life that treat me with the respect I deserve
- The rain that helps melt away the snow and bring spring a little closer
- Next week I have some free time out of school which will allow me to catch up on assignments
- My field placement at the beautiful Golden Year's Estate
- Another great day

SHEILA TRASK

Canada Blackberry

I believe that sometimes we don't try to move forward because we are afraid we won't succeed. We have the ability to do anything but sometimes we hold back. I am like this. I let fear control me like a puppet on a string. It pulls me away from pursuing my desires. I find myself in a rut, holding on and afraid to let go so that I can move forward with my life.

The day I gave birth to my son was the day I realized I was stuck. Fear was the first thing running through my mind and my body: fear of how life would change, fear that I wouldn't be a good mother, fear of losing friends, fear of losing myself and who I was. But when my son was placed in my arms, I felt nothing but gratitude. I knew I had to let go of fear for my baby's sake. I realized my baby was part of me, so holding on to fear would be holding my baby back as well. I realized my love for my son was stronger than anything that fear could throw at me. I knew then that everything was going to be okay. Life was going to change, but not necessarily for the worse. There would be sleepless nights and hours of crying, but in the end it would all be good. My gratitude for my son helped me chase fear out of my life. It helped me let go and move forward so that I am able to enjoy this precious baby, and be a good mother to him. Letting go meant I could enjoy my baby, and he could play, explore, and learn to live.

I am grateful for…

- My baby boy
- Coconut shampoo

SHEILA TRASK

- Frozen bananas with chocolate

- My nieces, my girls

- My friends

- The water... when I look at the ocean, I feel my sorrows drifting away with the currents.

Teacher

Once you understand your emotions it becomes easier to heal, let go, and move on. This won't happen overnight, but it will happen. Struggling to survive is about struggling to understand. Sometimes it can help to remember someone who listened to you and showed they cared. Perhaps by being your friend they gave you the confidence you needed to get through a difficult situation or set higher goals for yourself. I'm grateful for the kindness of Peter Ryall, my neighbour when I was 19, who encouraged me and planted the seed in my mind that I could be more than I really believed was possible at the time.

We are all stuck on those crossbars of life at some point. We all experience pain and sadness. But we can move on. Letting go is very difficult until you make the decision to let go. Life is going to have its ups and downs. As Zig Zigler says, "Getting knocked down in life is a given; getting up and moving forward is a choice." Once we make that choice everything seems easier. Forgive those who hurt you. Be thankful for those who helped. Start fresh. It is never too late. Just think of all the things you have to be grateful for and they will give you courage to move forward.

I'd like to share a personal story about how changing my attitude toward a situation allowed me to move forward. In January of 2013, Sparky, my faithful canine companion for over 11 years, took sick and died. I was very close to Sparky and held her in my arms as she passed. A few months later I decided to get a puppy, because I thought getting an older dog might remind me of my loss. But to my surprise, my beagle Bella, as cute as she was, only made me miss Sparky more. I continuously called her Sparky and she continuously proved to me that she wasn't. She was very mischievous. She hoarded things and collected them for her basket. Bella's basket was her closet. Unlike Sparky, she wasn't interested in sleeping in it or even napping in it. If I emptied the basket, she filled it up again. I never really understood what it was about.

Then one day I thought, something has to change. I was so miserable. I knew if I wanted to accept this dog, I had to stop expecting her to be Sparky. I had to let go of Sparky in order to be open to Bella. Once I understood this and changed my thinking, I grew to love Bella for her own unique personality. It was only then that I began to heal from the grief of losing Sparky. Instead of being angry with Bella and regretting getting her, I began to laugh at her antics and enjoy her mischievous and crazy personality. It was a chance to start over with gratitude. Animals teach us about people. They teach us how to love, accept, and forgive people, and, most importantly, how to appreciate and be grateful for them. Bella taught me how to move forward.

When we use gratitude to open ourselves up to life, we awaken the joy and beauty around us. Being grateful comforts and reassures us. When we feel safe and secure, it is easier to take risks, to let go of the cross bars. When gratitude is flowing in our lives, we learn to appreciate not only material things like a house or a car, but also the things we often take for granted such as our eyesight, the use of our limbs and our own special qualities. When we are grateful for all we have, it is easier to move forward, to reach for new goals.

Challenge Yourself

For one week keep track of habits, values or beliefs that may be holding you back. What beliefs do you have that are not true? What values do you have that are not serving you? What habits do you have that are not helping you? An example would be "I procrastinate". What can you do to change it?

Life Lessons Journal

Please go to **Part IV Life Lessons Journal** at the end of the book to complete the questions on this life lesson or go to **www.sheilatrask.com** to print off your own journal.

- LESSON FIVE -

DO SMALL THINGS
WITH GREAT HEART

"Not all of us can do great things, but we can do small things with great heart."

~ Mother Teresa

As a student I'll call Orach shows us, giving is not about the size of the gift. Orach's grandmother taught her that anything we give should come from the heart. To me this means you have to give for the right reason. Sometimes we can get too caught up in buying an expensive gift or making a grand gesture just to impress someone or to reassure ourselves that we have given or done enough. If we put our egos aside, it is easier to see what someone truly needs. Then we can give for the sake of giving. The value is in the act, not the price tag.

Orach

I was raised to believe that we should do onto others as we would have them do unto us. Love thyself, and love thy neighbour. Yes, spirituality was big in my home. I was taught from an early age to strive, achieve, and believe, in order to be the best that I can be. This gave me incentive to do my best, but sometimes it placed a great load on my shoulders, as I felt everything had to be perfect.

My grandmother, who was a very important person in my life, passed away in 2008. Her memory lives on in everything I do. She is with me in spirit. She taught me a lot, sometimes by reading me some of the inspirational quotes she collected. Since her death, I have struggled in many ways, and sometimes I forget the good things that I learned from my grandmother. Things like appreciating the simple things, believing in myself, and never letting others bring me down.

Recently I found my grandmother's little book of quotes, and it has been inspirational for me in so many ways. It's brought back the feelings I experienced reading those quotes with my grandmother when I was a child. She believed everyone should strive to be a good person by helping others. She always said that even the smallest gesture will mean a lot if you do it with a smile and if you are genuine. If you're genuine when you do something small for someone, it will mean just as much as giving them the moon. I guess she meant doing something with a good heart, no matter how big or small, is important.

This quote from Mother Teresa was one of my grandmother's favourites. It is like my grandmother speaking to me. Mother Teresa was a little woman with a big heart, who did everything she could for some of the poorest people, even if it was just a kind word, a touch, or a hug. My grandmother was a genuine person just like Mother Teresa and people still remember her and talk about her today. When I see someone who knew her, a conversation always begins about how sweet and genuine she was, and what a great heart she had. I hope that all of you believe that we can do great things by doing small things with great heart.

Teacher

Doing things from the heart is often the difference between making a difference and making a statement. Once I saw an elderly woman in a restaurant with a younger couple. They were being very impatient with her, repeatedly asking if she wanted this or this or this. She was very confused and I felt sorry for her. The quote reminds me of this episode. As I was leaving, the couple went up to order the food. I made a conscious effort to walk slowly by the elderly woman as I left. She was sitting there looking like she hated being a bother to anyone. I stopped and gave her a big smile. Her whole face lit up. I smiled again and then went out the door. I felt a huge connection with this woman. Her sadness seemed to lift as I smiled at her. This was not a big thing to do, but I believe it brightened her day. If you pay attention to other people, you may be able to make a small gesture that will make a huge difference in their day.

Here are some stories from the other wildflowers.

LIFE LESSONS
FROM THE WILDFLOWERS

Amaranth

I feel this quote can teach everyone a very valuable lesson. It means we all have different gifts to give the world. Regardless of our abilities, it is very important to do things with great heart and compassion. We often feel pressured to be perfect, to give the most, and to give the greatest gifts. We sometimes purchase gifts beyond our means, just to impress or keep up with others. Perhaps you want to do something special for someone; as long as it is a genuine gesture it doesn't have to be big. I admit that sometimes I have forgotten the true meaning of doing things with heart. I've worried, "Is this good enough?" Sometimes when I've received a gift I've wondered "How much did they spend?" Those things shouldn't matter. What really matters is giving from the heart. Little things like holding a door, smiling at someone, or letting someone go ahead of you in the checkout lineup are kind gestures that cost nothing, but can make someone else's day. I know that when someone does something for me, it makes me feel great.

During the class discussion, Teacher shared how she gave her father a handwritten letter as a birthday gift. She listed all the little things she remembered he had done for her and said thank you for each one. I think this is a wonderful gift. I have cards from my father and other family members that have passed. Every now and then I will read them and study their handwriting. It makes me feel closer to them and for that I am very thankful.

I am grateful for...

- My small group of friends. One in particular is always there to encourage me and listen when I need to talk. I am always there for her as well. We are very open with each other and are brutally honest when we need to be. We have each other's best interests at heart and our honest conversations have given us insights into things we may not have realized otherwise.

- I am so thankful I am able to visit my sister and her family in New Brunswick. I am grateful our relationship that has improved and we have become closer. My sister and I now have the special bond sisters should share. Her children bring me great joy and love. My nieces and nephew will always have a special place in my heart.

- A couple years ago, my uncle came back to Newfoundland and Labrador for the first time in almost 30 years. I had never met him. Although the circumstances that brought him back were sad, I am thankful that I had the opportunity to meet him and get to know him.

- Living in NL. We are very fortunate to live in such a beautiful place, not having to worry about starvation, clean water, or living in a war zone. Just look around, there is so much to be thankful for.

Arrowhead

This quote and the story the student told about her grandmother brought tears to my eyes, and inspired me. She spoke with pride and love. The simplicity of this quote holds much meaning for me. When I read it I thought of how for the past ten years I've wanted to be a nurse to help underprivileged children. I thought I was reaching for something unobtainable. I realized what I really wanted to do was to help people. Small acts of kindness build and can create a chain reaction helping people become kinder and more compassionate towards each other. I think the meaning of this quote is to forget the size of the deed and just do something to help. If you hold a door for someone with a bag of groceries or if you smile at someone who looks sad, you can brighten their day.

I am grateful for…

- My brain, and the ability to use it for the right reasons
- My heart, to feel compassion for others
- My eyes, to see the beauty life offers
- My province, living in Newfoundland and Labrador
- My food, to nourish my body

Barron Strawberry

The small acts of kindness we do for others can have more power and significance than we will ever know. Small acts of kindness done with love have the power to transform someone's world. They encourage others to also act with love and kindness. Something as simple as buying someone a cup of coffee can mean a great deal to someone, especially if they are not used to being treating with kindness. A small gesture has the power to move someone in a positive way. It really is about gratitude.

My mother spent years making breakfast for my brother and me. She wanted us to start the school day with a warm breakfast in our bellies, prepared to learn. Now, as an adult, I sometimes get up early (pretty early considering when my mother is up) to make her breakfast. I feel that since she did so much for others, it's time for her to experience how great it feels to have someone care enough to make you breakfast. Having a good heart does not mean you need to sacrifice or become overwhelmed. Do as many little things as you can. All the little things you do will make a difference in someone's life. Give what you can, no matter how small, just give with your heart. As Mother Teresa said, "If you can't feed a hundred, then just feed one."

I am grateful for...

- My classmates I share my days with
- For the courage to get up every day and go to school
- For all our earthly beauties
- For my hands so I can hold the hands of people I love
- The snow because it makes winter beautiful

Teacher

Gratitude begets giving. When people are grateful for the good things in their lives, they are more likely to give to others. When you give with gratitude you receive gratitude. Giving is not just about material gifts. A small gesture such as a simple hug can mean a great deal. Most of us think we should give because it makes others feel good. But giving is about balance. Sometimes we spend so much time giving that we are uncomfortable receiving. It's important to realize that by accepting a gift or a kind gesture you are honoring the person who is giving.

My mother was a great inspiration in my life. As an adult, I wanted to show her my gratitude for the many things—great and small—she had done with great heart. In 1998, my son was born on Mother's Day. My mother told me she knew I was in labour when she didn't hear from me. Mine was always the first of the ten calls she received from her children on Mother's Day.

I named my son after her father as a Mother's Day gift to her. When I came back to Newfoundland in 2001, I promised myself I would never miss being with her on Mother's Day. Despite my promise, one year I couldn't make it home. Although I didn't know it at the time, it would be her last Mother's Day. Recently my sister gave me a letter she found among my mother's things.

It was a letter I wrote my mother that year. I couldn't find the card I'd bought for her and I was afraid she wouldn't have a card from me. I found a blank card with a picture of a woman wearing the fanciest of clothes: a gorgeous dress, a fur scarf, and a beautiful black hat that hid her face. The card reminded me that my mother had sacrificed for her children. She never had fancy clothes and often did without to ensure we were clothed and fed.

My mom always wanted to have a career. When I graduated from university she said she felt she had not accomplished anything in her life. I told her she most certainly had. She'd found her blessing and purpose in raising her family. She was the person she had been born to be.[11] When I sent my mother the card, I enclosed this handwritten letter, the letter my sister found and returned to me.

---

[11] *Who I was Born to Be* by Susan Boyle was a song that represented my mother well. My sister Isabel and I played it for her in the hospital. It felt appropriate as Isabel, the eldest daughter, and I, the youngest daughter, each held one of her hands while the song played. She passed later that day.

Mom,

I know this is a different Mother's Day card, but I'm sending it for a reason. Just picture your head on this dress. That's how you are supposed to look and feel when you receive an award. Mother's Day is a day to celebrate the women who gave life to the world. If there was an award for this day, you would surely be the recipient. Giving birth to ten children is a major accomplishment. Giving ten outstanding citizens to the world is an outstanding achievement: six women who have well-paid careers in professions that allow them to help make the world a better place and four sons who also have celebrated careers whereby they provide for their families and benefit the community as well. The strengths we share as a family have been molded from the strengths of our Mother, one who knew that you had to hold strong, pick up for yourself, and survive. We all know that we have to put our children first and ensure that they grow up to be good, honest people. Having lots of money is not what makes people happy. The love of your children and the sense of accomplishment you feel when your children do well, that's priceless. I am sorry I wasn't there on Mother's Day this year. It is the first one I missed since I came back. But you taught me that I have to be there for my child, and as much as he told me to go, that I could leave him and miss his competition, I couldn't. When leaders in the community say I have a well-mannered son, I feel good. He says I taught him well. I know that people always said that about your children. We were raised with good values: to respect others, to be honest and hardworking, and, most importantly, to always do the right thing. Well that is what I'm trying to do today. The right thing is to tell my Mom thank you for always being there even when I didn't deserve it.

SHEILA TRASK

Thank you for guiding me and teaching me to believe in myself. Thank you for taking me on the train to visit Nan and Pop so I could have that special memory. Thank you for understanding when I tried and failed. Thank you for celebrating my accomplishments. Thank you for giving me life, and showing me how to live it right. It's taken 50 years to finally get it and to understand that happiness is within you. You have to love yourself. Be happy, be grateful, and never fear, as you are blessed. We are here to do all the things that you have done for us, all the things that you have taught us. I hope you had a Great Mother's Day, as you truly deserved it. I guess sometimes it pays to lose your card.

Thanks, Mom, you are wonderful and I love you very much.

Love,
Your daughter

Sheila

XX

P.S. I am very proud of you and I know you would look beautiful in this dress, accepting your award for Mother of the Year.

For Orach, finding her grandmother's book of quotes after her passing was a special gift, especially because she has memories of discussing the quotes with her. It's a gift that will continue to give Orach inspiration and comfort. I am grateful to have received the card that I gave my mother. I am grateful to her for having kept it. Another of my prized possessions is a painting my son did when he was in preschool. He was so proud of it that I framed it and hung it on the wall. It is called, "My Mom Looking at Me." I look at it and I smile.

Challenge Yourself

I think many of us would benefit from reading Eckhart Tolle. He writes that living in the present is really all we have. If we could just learn to stay here in the now, focusing on today, not tomorrow or the past, we would all be a lot happier and have fewer regrets. All the little things we can do for others can truly change their day and their lives. On a friend's birthday, make them a card, write them a poem, or sing them a song. These precious things make us feel special.

Life Lessons Journal

Please go to **Part IV Life Lessons Journal** at the end of the book to complete the questions on this life lesson or go to **www.sheilatrask.com** to print off your own journal.

- LESSON SIX -

STAY STRONG, STAY POSITIVE

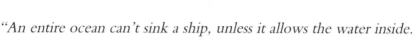

*"An entire ocean can't sink a ship, unless it allows the water inside.
Just as the negativity of the world can't drag you down unless you
allow that negativity inside! Stay strong, stay positive."*

~ Goi Nasu

I dedicate this lesson to a friend of mine who is a cancer survivor. She lives like no one else I have ever known. I hope she always maintains her positive attitude about life. She gives people hope, love, and prayers, even when she is the one in need. She is a testament to the fact that if you want love you must give it. She checked on other friends who were battling cancer the same time she was to offer them encouragement and love. In turn, hundreds of people sent her messages of love and encouragement on Facebook. She posted positive messages, she walked us through her treatments with pictures and humour, and she sang her way through chemotherapy and radiation. If you want to survive, you must act like a survivor. She counted down the days for her treatment in a way that made us laugh, cry, and smile, making us all feel like a community sharing her illness and cheering her on. I learned a lot from her when she was battling cancer. I learned having the right attitude goes a long way especially when you are fighting for your life. I am confident that she was the dream patient for the medical staff. She is an inspiration to the world. Joan Carroll-French—this one's for you. I am grateful for your positive attitude.

Fireweed, the student who chose this quote, developed a positive attitude and learned to be grateful for the good in her life during the semester she made this presentation.

Fireweed

Sometimes I feel I have experienced too much loss in my young life, but I am starting to have a new-found appreciation for the things loss can teach us about life and about ourselves. Loss often brings about change. How we react to these changes helps shape us into who we are meant to become. Regardless of our wants and desires, some of the things that happen are going to be bad. Life is a journey, so buckle up and enjoy the ride. I find inspiration in hearing stories about people who don't give up when they find themselves in difficult situations. It helps me view challenges as opportunities and reminds me to always make the best of what I have.

Recently Teacher handed back a piece of work I submitted, with a comment saying, "The sky is the limit for you." It's such a great feeling when someone gives you a compliment. We should try to say something positive to people who need our encouragement. It can make their day and help them continue their fight.

For me, this quote is telling me to stay positive. Your mind can be your best friend or your worst enemy. If you train your brain to think in a positive way, you will always find the good in the bad. A positive attitude is powerful, as are negative thoughts. Negativity can destroy your attitude and your perception, and make your mind a scary place.

Once we are able to focus on the positive, we can learn the lessons we need to from our experiences in life. Surrounding ourselves with positive people will help us maintain a healthier lifestyle. Negativity is contagious, and as much as we may love people in our life, if they are negative, they can pull us down. Sometimes the most difficult thing to do is weed out the negative around us, and that might include people.

Adopting a gratitude attitude means moving full steam ahead in life, filling it with positive experiences, positive people, and appreciating what you have. There is something positive in everything—we just have to look for it. My new attitude will allow me to see things that I never saw before. I realized that gratitude was the answer to any question I might have in life.

I am grateful for…

- My future. Although I'm not exactly sure where I will end up, I feel I am on the right track for success.

- My friend's little boy named Seth (Sethy). I am grateful for the opportunity to have him in my life. He has given me a better understanding of autism. Although he is unable to talk, he always has a special way of communicating and showing his love for me. Sethy is a special boy and no matter what challenges he faces, he is always happy and genuinely content. His display of love warms my heart and makes me feel special.

- My friend Melissa who out of the blue told me I was beautiful. That made my day and made me feel great. Just the confidence boost I needed.

- A new place to go. Melissa and I went to a new coffee shop today called the Jumping Bean. It has a nice, calm, and relaxing atmosphere and it's a great new place to hang out.

Teacher

Life is many things and it all goes back to my Mother's quote, "Life is how you see it". Everything has opposites: good-bad; happy-sad; positive-negative. We get to choose our outlook in life. We need to focus on the present and head forward. The past cannot be changed, so close that door and live for today. This new perspective has helped many students move forward in life. Let's hear what lessons these positive wildflowers have to share.

LIFE LESSONS
FROM THE WILDFLOWERS

Bed Straw Bell Flower

Ever since I was young, I have loved being on and near the ocean. Sailing with my uncles and grandfather has left me great memories of my time at sea. The boat is comparable to the body, mind and spirit. We can fill it with positivity or we can sink it with negative thoughts and emotions.

I am grateful for...

- Good health
- Being free of sickness
- A positive attitude
- The ability to learn new things
- The ability to read and write

Evening Primrose

The key to happiness is the gratitude attitude. If you focus your energy on what you have rather than what you don't, you will realize that you have a lot. Don't let your wounds transform you into someone you are not. We all have a past. We all make mistakes and we all have been mistreated at some point or another. Being grateful for what you have helps you have a positive attitude. This is what helps us cope, live each day to the fullest, and be our best.

I am grateful for

- Happiness
- My life
- My health
- My family
- My friends

Flat Top White Aster

I get stressed very easily, so I have found things to help get me through stressful situations. Music is one of them. I enjoy playing and listening to music and on my phone I have a playlist to help me cope with pretty much anything. Another thing I like to do is go snowmobiling. It's freedom. As I go along the trails, the wind takes away every care in the world, and when I reach my destination the view is awesome. Those are some of the things that help me stay positive and stay strong. That's life. With the right attitude it can be great. You have to appreciate all of those things you enjoy. Be grateful for your hearing so you can listen to music. Be grateful for the snow so that you can experience the wind in your face and the view from the top of the hill.

I am grateful for...

- Good health
- Being able to do things I enjoy
- People like Beck Smith
- People who smile at me on a blue day.

Teacher

When I think about what it means to stay strong and stay positive, I think about my childhood friend Cindy. I would like to share a story that happened recently and meant a lot to me. It comes to mind when I think of strength and how we have to dig deep to find it.

I was in Stephenville last summer, walking on the beach at Port Harmon. I love the ocean, and I was enjoying feeling the breeze as I walked beside the water collecting rocks. When I looked over to my van, I noticed that I had left the side door open, despite having locked all the doors. I figured I better get back over there, as I'd left my purse and my phone in the vehicle. When I checked my phone, I noticed a strange number—as a missed call and a voice mail. I listened to the message. It was my friend Cindy. We had been neighbours and had hung out together in our early teens. Since I had last seen her, she had lost a child. Surprisingly, when I called her back and asked her where she was, she said on the beach in Stephenville. We met up and shared a great couple of days together, walking on the beach and collecting rocks.

We picked up where we had left off—over forty years before—as if no time had passed. We brought up shared memories and filled in the gaps in the intervening years. We had lived a world apart for so many years, and we felt blessed to have this precious time together. It was perfect for both of us. We didn't feel pressure to talk all the time. We didn't ask questions of each other. We shared what we wanted to and the rest didn't matter. I am grateful for the time we spent together. The gift of friendship is truly priceless. We stayed strong and we stayed positive.

Challenge Yourself

The next time you are thinking negatively, say 'STOP'. Take your negative thoughts and replace them with positive thoughts. Look for the good in everything. If Joan could sing her way through chemo, you can find a positive thought. Being grateful will help you with your search. "… Stay strong, stay positive."

Life Lessons Journal

Please go to **Part IV Life Lessons Journal** at the end of the book to complete the questions on this life lesson or go to **www.sheilatrask.com** to print off your own journal.

- **LESSON SEVEN** -

EVERY SONG ENDS. IS THAT
ANY REASON NOT TO
ENJOY THE MUSIC?

"Whether it fades out or crashes away,
every song ends. Is that any reason not to enjoy the music?"

~ Ellie, One Tree Hill

Gratitude helps you enjoy the music. It helps you experience the journey with wondering eyes and an open heart. When you have a child, you begin seeing the world through a child's eyes. You develop a whole new appreciation for each moment. In the same way, cultivating a gratitude attitude can help you develop a new appreciation for the sights and sounds, the events—big and small—you encounter throughout your life.

Common Burdock is a young woman who has lost many loved ones in her short life. In her presentation, she tells us how she uses gratitude to focus on the good memories rather than dwell on her losses. Her positive attitude allows her to appreciate her life day by day.

Common Burdock

This quote represents an important lesson I learned in life. I will never forget my first day of high school, as that was the day I lost a good friend. In the next few years I continued to lose people I cared about. I realize now that I started focussing on their deaths and death in general. Life is about more than death. I realized that I needed to focus on the beautiful lives I had shared. I'm grateful for having had the opportunity to spend time with such wonderful people. I learned that you should never take life for granted, and that you should live life to its fullest.

When my friend died, that was a wakeup call for me. It was God telling me that I should be doing more of the things that make me happy. I learned that everything around me is precious. This experience helped me get my life on track and restored my faith in God. I am so grateful for those blessings in the midst of such a painful time.

Being grateful helped me look at things a little differently. For example, when my aunt and uncle died, I met family members that I had never heard of, and grew closer to relatives I already knew. This taught me a lesson: enjoy life and enjoy the ride. I am so grateful for having the opportunity to grow my relationships and gain new ones.

Since I was 3 years old, my father has been taking me for rides on his bike. Whether it was sunny or cloudy, morning or afternoon, I was always his little riding buddy. He took me everywhere he could think of, just to put a big smile on my face. As I got older, I think he thought I was too old to go for a ride. But that was far from the truth. I've never told him, but I enjoyed the rides so much because it gave us father daughter bonding time. Just remember: whatever you do, enjoy it. And tell those you love that you enjoy the time you spend with them.

Teacher

This quote reminded me of how students often forget to enjoy their time at college. Often they are so focused on the diploma that they miss out on the other things college has to offer. Participating in the gratitude project helped them understand the importance of making friends, having fun, and enjoying the learning process. They began to realize the importance of establishing balance in their lives. It's not only about getting an A, it's also about learning more about life and enjoying the journey. Now let's hear from some of the wildflowers.

LIFE LESSONS
FROM THE WILDFLOWERS

Creeping Buttercup

Life is what we make it. We can see the bad things and focus on negativity, or we can live with a smile and see the positive. Too many people work their lives away ignoring the fact that life is short, but it is important to stop and relish the little things. I was so caught up in trying to get A's in school, I forgot how important it was to spend time with the most precious thing in my life—my child—until one day he said to my cat, "Leave Mommy alone, she's busy." I realized I was so caught up in my schoolwork that I was missing out on my little boy. You only get to experience things once in your life, and watching your child grow and learn new things is very special. Now my life is about living slowly, enjoying every breath, and experiencing everything life has to offer. I truly am grateful for each and every moment.

I am grateful for…

- My son
- Music
- Owning a car
- Having money
- Having a house

- Living in a free country

White Clover

Life is a ride that can be joyous if you so choose. There was a time when I wasn't enjoying the ride because there were too many bumps in the road, but when I decided to take a detour, it brought great things into my life: things I had not seen, had never done, and still have left to do. Just this past weekend, my partner and I were in the woods cutting firewood. It's great exercise but it can also be hard work when you're up to your knees in snow and trying to carry sticks of wood to the road. As I was stomping through the snow, carrying wood and loving every minute of it, my partner said to me, "Oh my, the things we have to do." I looked at him and said, "It's not the things we have to do, but the things we choose to do." I am so filled with gratitude for the things we choose to do because we enjoy them together.

I am grateful for...

- My legs that let me walk through the woods to enjoy nature and all its beauty
- For the detour I took in the road that brought great things into my life
- Having all the riches in the world: health, love, and laughter
- Being my father's daughter, because he taught me the importance of respect
- Every day I get to live.

Moss Campion

This is a beautiful quote. Many good things and situations in life come to an end, but there is no reason not to enjoy them while they are happening. Look at every ending as an opportunity to learn, a new beginning. If you live in a world of fear and don't overcome your insecurities, you will miss out on wonderful things in life. Having a grateful attitude allows you to enjoy life to the fullest. Carpe Diem... seize the day.

I am grateful for...

- Going to the gym three times a week makes me feel fantastic. Having more physical strength and mental clarity makes me feel healthier, both physically and mentally. Working out is also a great way of releasing frustration.

- Being free of the addiction of smoking. My sinuses have improved and I find it easier to breathe.

- The joy of dancing. There is nothing I enjoy more than a night out with girlfriends, dancing the night away.

- Being feminine. I am a 'girly girl' at heart and feel great when I do my hair and make-up.

- Being free and not having to fight for gender equality the way women did in the past.

- Being ALIVE. I am thankful for every day, for the present, and for every opportunity. I cannot wait to see what the future holds for me, but I am thankful every day for the journey to get there.

Marsh Bedstraw

Life is about beginnings and endings. Even if something ends badly, that doesn't mean the experience was all bad. How you get to the destination is significant. I believe real learning happens through the means by which we travel. We gain wisdom through our experiences along the way. I believe that when we are fully present in the moment and feel grateful for what we are experiencing, our intuition is heightened and we are open to receiving guidance from the universe.

I am grateful for…

- The ability to self-reflect
- Having food to eat when I am hungry
- My health
- An intelligence that allows me to enjoy the world

Birdsfoot Trefoil

All good things must come to an end. You can't have a story without an ending. For me, an ending to a story is exciting because it just means a new story begins. I am grateful for the ability to write my own story.

I am grateful for...

- Beautiful sunny days
- Hearing the sweet sound of children's laughter
- My supportive family
- Another day of good health

Teacher

Gratitude opens us up, allowing us to see more opportunities in life. Spending less time on work and household demands and using some of that time to CONNECT with those we love is a great way to energize, physically and mentally. A great example of this is the time I recently spent with my son Jacob painting my friend Tamara's fence. Jacob and I connected just like my friend Cindy and I had on the beach. It is amazing how moments of silence and light conversation can be purposeful and gentle for our souls; no pressure, just enjoying the time you have together.

Practising the Gratitude Attitude allowed me to discover the joy in a simple event, turning it into a beautiful experience that filled my heart. My friend Tamara hired my son Jacob to paint her fence. It was a huge job. The fence was long, and Jacob had never done anything like this before. It made me proud, sad, happy, and excited to see just how much doing this task well meant to Jacob. I was so proud of him for trying and so grateful to my friend Tamara for letting him tackle this job. The winter had been a long and difficult one for my son. He had gone through his first breakup, and our previously close mother/son relationship had been strained. I had raised Jacob mostly as a single mother, and this new distance was very difficult for me.

While he was working, I'd visit Jacob to bring him food, hoping he would let me help. I felt so grateful when—after several days—Jacob finally opened his heart and allowed me to spend time helping him paint. I watched as his confidence increased. He said "Mom, I think I'm getting the hang of it now. It's going faster." I saw him visualize the finished job, as he talked about the progress he had made and how much more he had left to do. He was so proud of himself, and I felt closer to him than I had in a long time. I will cherish this memory forever, especially since we'd had such a challenging year trying to find the balance between us. Being a teenager can be difficult, but, as many parents will tell you, being the parent of a teen can be difficult as well. Watching your child grow up and experience life by making mistakes can be challenging. Teens need to feel independent and parents need to let go. It requires a lot of give and take to balance that parent-teen relationship. I am so grateful for the opportunity we had to paint that fence together. This experience recharged my gratitude attitude enough to carry me through the summer.

Challenge Yourself

Connecting is about whatever that means for you and the other person. It may be a simple hello, but it also may be sitting in silence, hugging, or working on a joint project. Sometimes life gets us down but we can find ways to connect. Here are a few suggestions to help you connect with those you care about.

Start a project together (don't try this at home). What I mean is that it is easier if you do it away from home as the dynamics change and the cooperation is much better.

Walk together.
Take on a charitable cause.
Clean up the neighbourhood or a favorite path.

Allow silence, as it is important when connecting to just allow things to be what they are; it should feel effortless. Let it unfold.

Plant flowers, wash the dog, find a box of memories, or create new memories.

Life Lessons Journal

Please go to **Part IV Life Lessons Journal** at the end of the book to complete the questions on this life lesson or go to **www.sheilatrask.com** to print off your own journal.

- LESSON EIGHT -

EVERY BREATH IS A REBIRTH

"With every in breath you are adding to your life and every out breath you are releasing what is not contributing to your life. Every breath is a re-birth."

~ **Allan Rufus,** *The Master's Sacred Knowledge*

Rebirth is an opportunity to get it right. If you really want to have the life you were born to have, you need to decide what you want from life. Ask yourself: What am I passionate about? What is my purpose in life? What changes do I need to make to make me feel whole?

This next student, Wild Lily of the Valley, literally and figuratively decluttered her life as a way to begin anew. Her level of self-awareness is admirable. Through self-discovery she learned just what she had to do to feel balanced and live in harmony.

Wild Lily of the Valley

Rebirth for me is about decluttering my life. As I looked back over my journal entries, I concluded that my life was chaotic, and I had no one to blame but myself. When I recently moved, I took the opportunity to establish a new beginning. I literally took the trash out of my life. I decided to stop creating problems for myself, to choose what I need each day and pitch the rest. It's like collecting dust. It feels good when you wipe it away.

The first thing I decided to do was to get to know myself. I asked, "What makes me tick, and what makes me feel good?" The first step in getting to know myself was to figure out my goals, and then write them down and create a plan to achieve them. I learned that if I don't do this, I will never accomplish anything, and I'll just feel frustrated. When I set myself up for failure like that, I create anxiety for myself. Unless I create goals and make plans, my life will continue to be stressful. So goal setting is now a priority for me.

The second thing I decided to do was to declutter my house, both literally and symbolically. Getting to know myself allowed me to adopt a new way of living. I learned that in order to think clearly and feel calm, I must live in a serene environment. I have also learned the importance of allowing myself "me time." I need to take time to do the things I like to do. My new choice of lifestyle is one of peace and serenity.

The third thing I decided to do was to spend five minutes each day sitting in silence. I have realized this year that I hate noise. I'm really irritated by noise pollution: dogs barking, babies crying, TVs blaring, cars honking, fridges buzzing, cats meowing... I could go on and on. I've learned that by taking some time to sit in a quiet room, I can rejuvenate. When I'm feeling calm and refreshed, I can cope with and even appreciate those sounds of daily life again.

It's also been very important for me to acknowledge that moving won't help me if I take the same negative energy with me to my new home. My new rebirthed energy will go with me wherever I go.

I am grateful for...

- The quiet
- The mornings
- The evenings
- My clutter free house
- My clutter free life
- Colors
- The stars
- My sense of smell; I love lilacs
- Ice cream
- Movies

Teacher

Let's see what rebirth is for the other wildflowers.

LIFE LESSONS
FROM THE WILDFLOWERS

Ground Ivy

I love and approve of myself! I need to tell myself this every day as I begin this rebirthing process. For me, meditation plays an important role in rebirth. Breathing exercises are the foundation of meditation, not only as a platform for focusing attention, but also because breathing is at the core of what it means to be alive. Every breath is an opportunity to reinvent my life. I inhale the energies that strengthen me and exhale the ones that hold me back. This process gives me new possibilities. I cleanse myself by absorbing this nurturing wisdom. I think we need to use our breath for rebirthing, just as mothers use their breath during the birthing process.

I am a survivor. I will not allow myself to drown in sorrows. I will take the lessons learned and move on. This will transform me into someone I know I am; back to whom I am meant to be.

I am grateful for the opportunity to be born again. I know when I take a breath in and a breath out, it feels awesome! Live the life you love, and love the life you live.

I am grateful for...

- Happiness
- Strength
- My life
- People who care
- People who give me advice

Dandelion

Rebirth is being born again, starting fresh. It means looking at what you like and don't like about yourself. It also means facing your challenges and exploring beliefs that may be holding you back. One of my challenges is procrastination. There are things that everyone hates doing, whether it is housework or shoveling snow. But choosing to live by the motto "I'll do it later" means nothing will ever get done. Teacher has taught me that procrastination is about fear, the fear of making a decision. This got me to thinking about why I am afraid to make a decision. If I am going to be born again I need to make decisions.

Another thing I find challenging is facing people I have wronged and those who I feel have wronged me. I believed that once I had a falling out with someone, if they came back into my life, then it was meant to be; if not, then it wasn't. So I did nothing. I just waited to see what would happen. Now I understand that relationships, like dishes, require work. If I wait for those dishes to do themselves, they will linger. I can't escape the responsibility I have for my relationships; it follows me like a shadow. I've made a choice to take responsibility and reconnect with those I've wronged. With every sincere "I'm sorry" written and sent, I can feel myself becoming lighter. Regrets drag me down. Releasing those regrets enabled me to fly, live for today, and be grateful for the people in my life. Rebirth is easy once you are grateful for what you have. My new affirmation is, "I am an expression of rebirth."

I am grateful for...

- Chicken noodle soup
- Chinese food
- Clocks, as I like knowing how much time I have left in my day so I never waste a second
- Cooking
- Baking

Bur-Reed

Before entering the Community Studies Program, I found myself walking around angry at the world. Everyone I ran into was unhappy or mad or just plain rude; or so I thought. I had recently lost my mom and left a failed marriage, and I didn't know where to turn in life. I was in so much pain and grief that I found it hard to be happy. I tried to walk around with a smile, and not show the pain that I was feeling. I thought that if I came across as a positive, strong person then maybe someone else could gain strength from me. But how can anyone gain strength from anger and hate? If I'm in a bad romantic relationship or a bad friendship, I can't expect change to begin with the other person. I was sitting around waiting for the world and people around me to change. I had to become the person I wanted others to be.

Change begins with me—that's what I learned. I need to inspire those around me to do better, by modelling the behaviour I expect from others. That is rebirth to me. If we desire a world that has less anger and hate, we should interact with others in a kind and loving manner on a daily basis. When I started thinking about all the things I had to be grateful for, I realized that if I became happier with myself, I would start seeing joy and beauty in the world. It's all there. We just have to look for what we want. When we decide to behave as we would like others to behave, that behaviour can spread, just like the yawn in Dr. Seuss's Sleep Book.

I was raised to be grateful, but somewhere along the way I lost touch with gratitude. By starting to practice gratitude again and making it part of my daily life, I've started to become the change that is shaping my world into a more wonderful place. So like a caterpillar changing into a beautiful butterfly, I've begun to grow into the person I've always wanted to be. My mother would be so proud of me.

If I desire peace, I must be peaceful. If I desire joy, I must be joyful. If I desire generosity, I must give. I want the world to see me as a strong person; someone who will stand up for what I believe in and not let anyone walk over me. I want to be able to do things I enjoy. But I've learned that if I want a life I can be grateful for, I must be grateful for the life I have.

I am grateful for…

- The good people in the world
- Chocolate

- Good doctors
- People who care about the less fortunate
- A good laugh once in awhile

Alpine Azalea

Rebirth is the dance of life. In life it is important to dance to every song, not just the same song over and over. Sometimes our moves have to change because the rhythm changes, but we learn new steps as we go. Life doesn't end because a new song begins. It continues on.

The concept of rebirth reminds me of when I moved away from home for the first time. I was 19. I sat in the window of my new apartment and watched my parents drive away. I didn't know anyone, and I had just been diagnosed with epilepsy. I had no friends or family nearby. I was alone. I remember sitting there saying to myself "What am I going to do now?" I decided to get up and go for a walk. I walked until my feet hurt and I got lost. I was scared. When I finally found my way home, thanks to a police officer and his wife, I realized I was going to be okay. I had to change my thinking and my way of life. I had to start over and learn to live this new life that was in front of me. It was a new song, so I had to learn a new dance. The rhythm of life keeps us moving. Rebirth is positive; we have to be open to change.

I am grateful for...

- Cake
- My long hair
- School

- My teacher
- Candy
- My comfy bed
- Sunshine
- High heels

Teacher

My rebirth began at a defining moment in my life. When I turned 55, I realized that I had one chance to play the leading role in my life story. Up to this point I had focused on helping other people. Although that is not a bad thing, I realized I was always playing the supporting actress in my own life.

In 2015, after having read over 500 books on personal development, inspiration, motivation, professional development, and human development, and taking numerous courses and workshops, I decided that I wanted to be more and live more. By becoming an Educator I thought that I would be able to help people move forward in their lives. For many students I may have played that role, but during my teaching days, it struck me that I needed to make a huge change. I was no longer content to play the role of teacher. I wanted to be a mentor and work with people who seriously wanted to change their lives, not just get a diploma. I decided several things during that transformational period, including: one, I would finish writing the book you are holding in your hands; and, two, I would become reborn, creating my own company to offer consulting and coaching services.

I knew that after 30 plus years working and studying people I finally had it figured out. My passion for helping people was connected with my life purpose. I started thinking about what my Grade 11 homeroom teacher, Les Campbell, said to me back in 2002, when I went home for my father's funeral. I ran into Les in a bar where I'd gone with some of my family members to get a bite to eat and unwind. I hadn't seen Les since I'd graduated in 1977, but he told me he remembered me well as a student. I will never forget our conversation. He asked me if I was still out there fighting for the rights of other people, especially those who couldn't fight for themselves. He told me that what he remembered most about me was that I was always trying to change the world; that I never sat back and let things happen. I made them happen. This is still true to who I am today. Les has now passed but I am so grateful that I got the opportunity to hear that from him. It made me feel good to know that a former teacher remembered something so integral to who I am as a person.

I believe we need to be the change that we wish to see in the world. That saying is on my fridge for a very good reason. I wish to take action where I believe action is needed. I feel that way too many people sit back and complain without ever trying to change things. This leads me back to my rebirth. For the next half of my life— call it a midlife crisis, it does not matter—I wish to really be the change I'd like to see in others. I want to live this half of my life doing things a little differently. I want to focus on me more. I was raised to put others first. Today I understand that it is not selfish to do something for myself. Today I begin my life anew. I will do the things I love and steal my life back for me.

I was born to write, to teach, to learn, to speak. I know this because these are the things I love to do and time flies when I am doing any of them. The opportunity we all have is to think about the positive things we wish to keep and all the negative things we need to let go. The greatest crime would be to live our lives without ever finding out what we're truly meant to do. All the great writers have said this and they are all so right. Serena Dyer wrote a book with her father (Dr. Wayne Dyer) called Don't Die with the Music Still in You. Her father wanted his children to understand this more than anything. Ironically, it took his passing for me to understand this and take action. I think most of us would agree that while you still have a chance to find your passion and live it, you should do it. Seek what is seeking you. Do what you love and love what you do. These messages are consistent in everything I read. I need to dream as big as I can, as I never know where I will end up.

I am so grateful for...

- Learning that with every breath I take in I give myself new opportunity.

- Learning that every breath I breathe out gives me an opportunity to get rid of things that no longer serve me in my life.

- Having a midlife crisis that gave me the opportunity to re-examine my life and take it back for me.

- Understanding from John Kehoe, author of many books on the power of the mind, that a midlife crisis is the universe saying "Hey wake up and get it right. "What do you have left to do while you are here on earth?

- Understanding that a midlife crisis is rebirth: a chance to be born again; a chance to get it right!

Challenge Yourself

If you were given an opportunity to be born again what would you do differently? Begin your life today, take chances you normally would not take. Say yes when you mean yes and no when you mean no. Do something wild and crazy today that you wouldn't normally do. Breathe in as if it were your last breath and breathe out to the world as if it were your first.

Life Lessons Journal

Please go to **Part IV Life Lessons Journal** at the end of the book to complete the questions on this life lesson or go to **www.sheilatrask.com** to print off your own journal.

PART III

- FOREVER IN GRATITUDE -

"The landscape belongs to the person who looks at it."

~ Ralph Waldo Emerson

It is my hope that you have found comfort in this book. I hope that reading our Life Lessons has encouraged you to find gratefulness in your life, and that you will be inspired to view life in a new and more positive way: where all the little things become the precious things. I hope you look forward to more Life Lessons from the Field, as there are more to come. And as my Mother said in her last days, "Life is how you see it." Life really is about interpretation. Be grateful for your blessings.

I would now like to share with you my formula for finding gratitude and keeping it. Use your Life Lessons Journal to help you widen your perspective and sharpen your ability to take those little things and enjoy them. Let's learn to look, share, and recharge our gratitude.

CREATING THE GRATITUDE ATTITUDE

I created a process to help people turn on the flow of gratitude and keep it flowing. I call this the three step process: 1. Look, 2. Share, 3. Recharge. If you consistently practise these three steps, you will develop the Gratitude Attitude and keep it.

LOOK, SHARE, RECHARGE

I will explain each step and give examples to demonstrate the three step process for you.

STEP ONE: LOOK for gratitude in your life.

It is important to begin this process by simply looking. As the Bible says, "Seek and ye shall find." I looked at all aspects of my life: my personal life, my career, my physical surroundings, and the larger world around me. I found myself appreciating my family, my friends, my colleagues and all the other people who have played a role in my life, including those who have passed on. I even looked at myself.

Let me show you how I follow the process.

Gratitude is like love. You cannot truly love someone unless you love yourself first. Gratitude works the same way, you cannot truly be grateful for other people, if you're not grateful for your own life. Appreciating ourselves enables us to appreciate others. So I looked at myself and discovered some qualities for which I'm truly grateful. I am a kind person. I love to give and to help others. I throw myself into everything I do and give 100%. I always want to do my best and give my best. When I decide to do something, there is no stopping me. I am grateful that Bob Proctor of the Proctor Gallagher Institute recognized my passion and drive at a seminar last year. While I was diligently watching his presentation, taking careful notes, afraid to blink in case I missed something, Bob stopped in front of me and said, "You are like a dog with a bone." Everyone laughed but I smiled as I knew he had picked up on my thirst for knowledge and desire to do something with it. This hunger for success is what many call passion. I am grateful for my passion.

Next, I looked at my family. I am grateful for my son Jacob.

Once I recognized how kind, considerate, and sensitive he is, I started to focus on those traits instead of dwelling on his teenage moods. This makes me appreciate him more.

My parents, Effie and Gerard, now deceased, have taught me many things. My Mom taught me to be responsible. I feel grateful that she grew to understand me so well. I am grateful for my Dad: for his sense of humour, for being the fun and loving person that he was. He made us laugh and see the lighter side of life.

I am grateful for my nine brothers and sisters. I think working hard to compete within the tribe made me a better person. Despite our shortcomings, we know that blood is thicker than water, so watch out if you mess with any of us. I am grateful for my four brothers: Nelson and Aaron for their musical talent and the numerous hours of entertainment they provided us over the years; Leonard for his humour; and Melvin for stepping up to be head of the family after Dad passed. I am also grateful for my five sisters: Christina for caring for my parents in their later years; Philomena for being willing to try Mom's recipes so we could keep those memories alive; Jessie for the guidance she gave me as a teenager; Irene for the plane ticket she sent me so that I could come home for Mom's birthday in 1999; and Isabel, who is like a second mother to me, for taking the weekly calls I used to make to Mom. You see how easy it is to get that Gratitude Attitude flowing?

I looked at my work colleagues, my friends, and my other relationships. For example, I am grateful for my friend Andrea's perspective on life, which is often eye-opening because it is different than mine. I am grateful for Jennifer's kind demeanour; despite what she may be tackling in life, she is always nice to everyone. I am grateful that my supervisor Joan appreciates everything I do and understands the challenges we face in our work lives. I am grateful for Mireya, my reading partner (we read together by phone), who always makes insightful comments that make me think. I am grateful for Jason, my fitness trainer, who has whipped me into shape many times and helped me get my strength back after injuries. I am grateful for my hairdresser Natasha, who always listens to me blabber on and cuts my hair just the way I like it. I am grateful for Sam, who does my nails to perfection.

I also looked at the little things in life that are so easy to take for granted. I love the birds that gather in a tree in my yard. I am grateful for the songs they sing and the hours of entertainment they give me. I am grateful for my dog Bella and her endless hugs and kisses. I am grateful for the fresh snow that lights up the yard and the wind that keeps us from getting too hot in the summer. I love the rocks on the beach in my hometown of Stephenville. I love the heat from the fireplace on a wintery night. I am grateful and feel very blessed.

Identifying the blessings in your life, the good in everyone and everything, is just the first step. Next you need to act. You have to put the Gratitude Attitude to work to get it flowing. So I decided to share my gratitude by showing people that I am grateful for them.

STEP TWO: SHARE your gratitude with others by consciously acting on it.

If you are grateful for the people around you, you need to make an effort to let them know. Imagine how great that would make them feel. First of all, I share my gratitude with my son Jacob by showing him how grateful I am to have him in my life. I act on this by telling him that I believe in him and support him, and trust him to be his best self. I allow him to make his own mistakes and take his own risks, knowing that I will be there to support him if he needs me. I have compassion for my son without trying to control him. I am grateful for him without trying to fix him.

You can let your family members know that you are grateful by doing small things. When you have a large family it is difficult to keep up with all the birthdays and anniversaries, but it's important to make an effort, even if it is just sending an email or saying Happy Birthday on Facebook. It is much better to tell someone you care in a phone call or an email, rather than saying it at their funeral.

I am blessed with many good friends, including my new friends, Paula, Jose, and Kay. I love getting together with my female friends to enjoy each other's company and share stories of our lives. We have laughed and cried together. No matter how long it is between our visits we just pick up where we left off. I am grateful for our differences; each of us is unique. I love my friends and I need to show them that I am grateful for our friendship. I can do that by ensuring we stay in touch on a regular basis through a phone call, a text, or a message on Facebook. Always make time for your friends;

otherwise they will not know you are grateful for them. Finally, tell them that you are grateful for them: say it out loud.

It's important not to take work colleagues or trainers or hairdressers for granted. If someone has performed a service well, let them know you are grateful by giving them a small token of your appreciation. Give them referrals. Tell them how good they are at what they do. Share your gratitude with the world.

If you look around you, you'll see lots to appreciate. Share your gratitude by looking after your garden and filling up the bird feeders. Walk your dog, play with her, and give her a bath. Water your plants and tell them they are beautiful. Respect your local beaches by keeping them litter free. We need to show our gratitude for our beautiful earth by never taking more than we need and always leaving something for someone else.

If all this seems a little overwhelming, don't worry. If you practise sharing your gratitude on a regular basis, it becomes a normal part of your daily life, of who you are. However, there are times when we all feel a bit down and need a pick-me-upper. That's why we need to recharge: to replenish our gratitude attitude.

STEP THREE: RECHARGE your Gratitude Attitude.

In order to maintain your gratitude attitude, you need to look after yourself mentally, spiritually, and physically. It's easy to be grateful when we're feeling healthy, contented, and safe, but life throws us all curveballs. When times are tough or we are feeling down, we need to dig deeper to tap into our feelings of gratitude. Any unexpected loss or discomfort may interfere with our gratitude flow. Think of a garden hose. The water runs freely from the hose once you turn on the tap, but if someone steps on the hose the water flow stops abruptly. The flow of gratitude is like this flow of water, and a crisis is like someone stepping on the hose. Everything comes to a halt. Having a Gratitude Attitude helps us continue to see life's blessings when times are tough or we are in crisis. To keep this feeling of gratitude flowing, ensure that you recharge yourself— physically, mentally, and spiritually.

There are several ways to do this.

Meditation is one of my favorite ways to recharge. If the idea of meditation seems foreign to you, begin by sitting still for five minutes a day in a quiet room. Relax: just listen to sounds that you might normally ignore such as the clock ticking, the birds singing, the fridge humming, or the dog breathing. When you're ready to learn to meditate, you can go to my website **www.sheilatrask.com** to find a complimentary meditation to help you get started.

Savor every sip of your first cup of morning coffee. It is the absolute best. I just sit and appreciate the taste. Not a coffee drinker?

Do it with whatever beverage you enjoy.

I love to get up early in the morning before anyone else is awake as this gives me the solitude I need to begin my day. I do my "gratituding" and read, meditate, or write. This is what feeds my soul. Whatever feeds your soul will recharge your Gratitude Attitude. There is Gratitude Pad on my website www.sheilatrask.com to help you with your `gratituding`.

Hug your pet. My beagle Bella loves to hug.

Go for a nature walk on a trail or by the water, or just stroll around town. I find it calming to observe the other living things that share my world. I've created a bird sanctuary in my back yard. I love to watch the many types of birds that come to feed there. I also get to watch the squirrel climb the tree to find the food I've left for it. This really feeds my soul.

Watch uplifting videos or listen to your favorite music. I love to listen to a manifestation video after my first cup of coffee. Listening to music or a meditation gets my creative juices flowing.

Visualize a favorite place. When I want to feel gratitude, I often think of the ocean in Stephenville. I love the smell of the ocean, the sound of the waves, the taste of the salt on my lips, and seeing the sun sparkle on the water. I remember the many discussions I've shared with close friends or family over the years as we walked the beach looking for white rocks to take back to my garden, to remind me of my hometown.

This, my friends, is what gratitude is about. See how easy it is to follow the three step process: to look, share, and recharge your Gratitude Attitude? Through looking you awaken the gratitude attitude, through sharing you increase it, and through recharging you build up the reserves you need to get through the tough days when you are stressed or overworked or life just gets you down. The more stress you have, the more sources of gratitude you need to recharge your attitude.

Once you follow the three step process, you may notice that your ability to appreciate the little things in life has been heightened.

Life Lessons Journal

Please go to **Part IV Life Lessons Journal** or go to **www.sheilatrask.com** to print off your own journal.

"*Although time seems to fly by, it never travels faster than one day at a time. Each day is a new opportunity to live your life to the fullest.*"

~ **Dr. Steve Maraboli**

LIVE EACH DAY TO THE FULLEST

As my father used to say, "We are only sure of today; yesterday is gone and we don't know if we have tomorrow, so it is very important to live each day as if it were our last." I guess he meant we should have no regrets. Say the things you want to say and do the things you want to do. My father was good at giving advice. He was wise in many ways. I remember so many of the things—big and little—he taught me. He said that when he worked in the fields, he learned that dew in the morning meant it was going to be a beautiful day. He used this example to encourage me to seize the opportunities I saw before me. You can't make hay when the sun isn't shining. He just wanted me and everyone else to live life to the fullest.

Parents pass many words of wisdom along to their children. If young people would only heed their parents' advice, they would avoid getting into many difficult situations. But, of course, it's easy to let it go in one ear and out the other. We have to learn the hard way. But as we get older, we realize they were right. My parents' greatest piece of advice was to live life to the fullest. My parents had little education. I believe my father went to work in the fields when he was nine, and my mother left home at age 14 to work "in service" with a family, but they always encouraged their children to get an education. They wanted more for us. They were so hell bent on pushing us into the world that they gave us each a luggage set as a gift when we graduated from high school. I remember mine, it was blue. I couldn't wait to fill those suitcases up and leave home. I couldn't fit everything I had accumulated into those three suitcases, but that was okay as I didn't go away for long periods of time until in 1983, after I'd been out of school for six years, I made the big announcement that I was going to university. I am sure my parents were glad. It isn't that I wasn't doing anything worthwhile; it was just that my parents really wanted me to go to university. My mother used to tell me I had brains to burn. I laugh when I think about that now. She had a lot of strange sayings. My father told me that an education would give me freedom and independence. That means more to me than anything, as freedom and independence are at the core of who I really am. I have to be free to me; not the "me" that you think I should be, but the "me" that I think I should be. It took me a long time to figure that out.

This final lesson is a poem called "Live Each Day to the Fullest" which I've transcribed from a plaque my parents gave me as a gift when I graduated from university. Recently, when I picked up the plaque and read the poem, I realized how significant its meaning has become for me. The poet isn't credited on the plaque, but while writing this book, I learned the poem was written by Jean Kyler McManus. I have adopted it as a daily prayer to remind me to live each day to the fullest and to always be grateful.

I am grateful for being able to share this with you!

Teacher

LIVE EACH DAY TO THE FULLEST

Yesterday's troubles
are written sand,
brushed out of existence
by God's own hand.

The things of the future
our hearts may fear,
can all be resolved
when tomorrow is here.

Out of a lifetime, these hours alone,
the hours of today
are completely our own.

So as each sun is setting,
there's reason to say,
"Thanks, Lord, for your gifts-
above all for this day."

~ Jean Kyler McManus

MY FINAL GRATITUDE

I am grateful for **Dr. Wayne Dyer,** who passed while I was writing this book, for the many lessons he taught me in life. I am grateful that I was able to tell him in person how much he has helped me. He has influenced me more than any other author or speaker, and through his work he has introduced me to many more inspiring minds.

I am also grateful for **Deepak Chopra,** for his many thought provoking books and tapes. Through his work I learned to meditate and to use meditation as a daily tool. **Eckhart Tolle:** I am grateful that through your work you taught me mindfulness. Learning to stay in the present helped me through the grief of losing my mother. I am also grateful for **Louise Hay,** as her work started me on this journey of seeking answers, loving life, and understanding the importance of positive affirmations.

And, finally, I would like to thank **Oprah Winfrey** for demonstrating the importance of believing in yourself, being confident and being real, and for helping so many people in this world through her OWN channel.

Although I have had other mentors, these mentors have led the way for me, and for that

I AM...
Eternally Grateful,

Sheila Trask
Teacher

PART IV

- LIFE LESSONS JOURNAL -

LESSON ONE: TALK ABOUT YOUR JOYS

*"Talking about our problems is our greatest addiction.
Break the habit. Talk about your joys."*

~ Rita Schiano

What was your greatest lesson today? Go to your journal and write how you feel about this quote. Here are some questions to get you thinking.

1. What was your greatest lesson today?
2. Do you talk about your problems?
3. If yes, why do you do so? If no, think about someone who does.
4. Why do you think he/she does this?
5. Does talking about problems change the mood of the conversation? Discuss how.
6. Write at least five things you are grateful for.

LESSON TWO: RISE FROM THE GROUND LIKE A SKYSCRAPER

"Go on and try to tear me down. I will be rising from the ground like a skyscraper..."

~ Demi Lovato

What was your greatest lesson today? Go to your journal and write how you feel about this quote. Here are some questions to get you thinking.

1. Write about a time when you felt like you were being torn down.
2. How did you react?
3. How would you react now that you have learned about self-love and self-esteem?
4. Would you do things differently?
5. Write at least five things you are grateful for.

LESSON THREE: WORRY CAUSES FEAR CAUSES WORRY

"We are, perhaps, uniquely among the earth's creatures, the worrying animal. We worry away our lives."

~ **Lewis Thomas,** *The Medusa and the Snail*

"The only thing we have to fear is fear itself."

~ **Franklin D. Roosevelt**

What was your greatest lesson today? Go to your journal and write how you feel about the quote. Here are some questions to get you thinking.

1. What does fear mean to you?
2. Think about a time when you were afraid. How did you feel? What were you afraid of?
3. Was the fear real? Why or why not? Explain.
4. If I told you that what you think about is more likely to happen would this change what you think about?
5. What kind of things can you think about to make you feel good and have good thoughts?
6. How can being grateful help you overcome worry and fear?
7. Don't forget to write at least five things that you are grateful for.

LESSON FOUR: YOU HAVE TO LET GO
TO MOVE FORWARD

"Getting over a painful experience is much like crossing the monkey bars. You have to let go at some point in order to move forward."

~ C.S. Lewis

What was your greatest lesson today? Go to your journal and write how you feel about this quote. Here are some questions to get you thinking.

1. Think of a painful time in your life when you had to make a decision to let go so that you could move forward. What did you do?
2. How long did it take you?
3. What was left for you to be grateful for?
4. Do you think that focusing on the good in your life would have made the situation different, perhaps even easier?
5. Write at least five things that you are grateful for.

LESSON FIVE: DO SMALL THINGS WITH GREAT HEART

"Not all of us can do great things, but we can do small things with great heart."

~ Mother Teresa

What was your greatest lesson today? Go to your journal and write how you feel about this quote. Here are some questions to get you thinking.

1. Think about something priceless you have given or received. Why was it priceless? Write all of the reasons you can think of. Was it because of who gave you the gift, the gift itself or the fact that it was given with great heart.

2. Do you have a memory that reflects this life lesson? Write about it. If not, create one. It is never too late to show those you love what is in your heart.

3. Pay tribute to someone you feel is deserving of recognition. Write them a letter, give them a handwritten card, sing them a song, or do whatever you feel best represents your appreciation. Write about the experience in your journal.

4. Write about all the gifts you are grateful for, big or small.

LESSON SIX: STAY STRONG, STAY POSITIVE

"An entire ocean can't sink a ship, unless it allows the water inside. Just as the negativity of the world can't drag you down unless you allow that negativity inside! Stay strong, stay positive."

~ Goi Nasu

What was your greatest lesson today? Go to your journal and write how you feel about this quote. Here are some questions to get you thinking.

1. Have you ever experienced a time when you felt you had to stay strong, stay positive? Discuss this experience.
2. What lessons did you learn from that experience? Keep in mind that lessons in life are often hidden in our sorrows, not in our moments of joy. We just don't know that at the time we are experiencing it.
3. What things could you do to help yourself and/or someone else during a time that you need to be strong?
4. What five things are you feeling grateful for today?

LESSON SEVEN: EVERY SONG ENDS. IS THAT ANY REASON NOT TO ENJOY THE MUSIC?

"Whether it fades out or crashes away. Every song ends. Is that any reason not to enjoy the music?"

~ Ellie, One Tree Hill

What was your greatest lesson today? Go to your journal and write how you feel about this quote. Here are some questions to get you thinking.

1. Reflect on a story of how you spent time with someone and it meant a lot to you. Who was this person? What did you do together? What made this time so special?
2. Is there someone in your life that you would like to spend time with? Create that special moment. Think of what you can do to make this happen. Write about it and how it made you feel. How did the other person feel?
3. What suggestions would you make to someone about enjoying the music? List what you think would make that music sweeter.
4. Write five or more things that you are grateful for.

LESSON EIGHT: EVERY BREATH IS A RE-BIRTH

"With every in breath you are adding to your life. And every out breath you are releasing what is not contributing to your life. Every breath is a re-birth.?"

~ **Allan Rufus,** *The Master's Sacred Knowledge.*

What was your greatest lesson today? Go to your journal and write how you feel about this quote. Here are some questions to get you thinking.

1. What does rebirth mean to you?
2. If you were to be reborn what would that look like?
3. What changes would you like to see in your life?
4. What steps can you take to make these changes happen?
5. What are you passionate about?
6. What do you think is your life purpose?
7. Remember, to bring about positive changes in your life, you need to appreciate what is already there. Always be grateful. What are the things that you are grateful for?

CREATING THE GRATITUDE ATTITUDE

In your journal, do the following three activities. This will help you create your Gratitude Attitude and keep it.

1. **Look** – Create a list of all the people, places, and things you are grateful for.

2. **Share** – For each person, place, or thing you have listed explore the ways you can show your gratitude. Write these down.

3. **Recharge** – List ways you can replenish your source. Make sure your list is long enough to keep your attitude flowing. What kinds of things feed your soul? You can never have too many sources, so be open to appreciating the new and unexpected. Record those when they happen. Remember that the more open you become, the more you will see and appreciate.

I have written a detailed example to show you how you can think about a person from your past and find unique ways to show them you are grateful for them. Here is a brief example to remind you of the process:

1. **Look** – I am thinking of Sheila Byrne who was my school nurse when I was a child. She was the kindest, sweetest nurse anyone could ask for. Going to see her—even if you were getting a vaccine—was a joy. She had the warmest smile and the kindest, most gentle way about her. Everyone loved her and had only good things to say about her.

2. **Share** – On October 10, 2015 she celebrated her 90th birthday. I asked her daughter Maureen to make a posting on Facebook so we could all give her birthday wishes and share stories. I was hoping she would get at least 90 happy birthday wishes in response to the posting. It didn't take long for the wishes to start coming in. There were too many to count. I wanted to share my gratefulness with Nurse Byrne and with her family as she had given so much to all of the school kids when we were growing up. She came to my Mom's funeral and that meant so much to me and to my family. As a child, I pretended I was named after her because I loved her so much.

3. **Recharge** – I listened to a meditation on relaxation before going to sleep. Just like putting my phone on charge.

LIVE EACH DAY TO THE FULLEST

Here's your final question.

1. What do you need to do to ensure you live each day to the fullest?

Answer - Always Be Grateful

ABOUT THE AUTHOR

Sheila Trask spends her time reading, learning, and discovering new ways to help others realize their full potential. She is an Educator, Personal and Professional Development Consultant and Coach, Motivational Speaker, and Community Activist. She is an instructor at the College of North Atlantic in Grand Falls-Windsor, Newfoundland and Labrador, Canada.

As a result of her own personal transformation, Sheila decided to share her passion for personal growth and development with the world so she founded her own company 1ST Choice Consulting. Sheila is a member of the Canadian Certified Coaches Federation and the first Thinking into Results Certified Consultant in Atlantic Canada for the Proctor Gallagher Institute. To learn more about Sheila go to **(www.sheilatrask.com)**.

"If I desire peace, I must be peaceful. If I desire joy, I must be joyful. If I desire generosity, I must give. I want the world to see me as a strong person; someone who will stand up for what I believe in and not let anyone walk over me. I want to be able to do things I enjoy. But I've learned that if I want a life I can be grateful for, I must be grateful for the life I have."

~ Bur-Reed, a wildflower from the field

Made in the USA
Las Vegas, NV
01 December 2021

35744678R00094